Israel
The Blessing
or the Curse

For biblical relevant news, please go to
www.watch.org

For additional studies about the Bible, please go to
www.branchofdavid.org

First Printing—November 2001
Second Printing—April 2002

All Scripture quotations are from the King James Version of the Holy Bible.

Printed in the United States of America

ISBN 1-57558-091-8

Israel

The Blessing

or the Curse

John McTernan & Bill Koenig

Acknowledgments

Bill Koenig would like to acknowledge and give thanks to:

- **Herschel Sanders** for his friendship, guidance, fellowship, and example. He is a true man of God.
- **Lee Fox** for his many hours of discipling during the early years of my Christian walk.
- **Pat Booth** for his friendship, guidance, fellowship, and boldness in sharing the Gospel.
- **Dr. Greg Rosener**, a true friend who came through in a time of great need. His passion for the Lord has impacted many people's lives.
- **Butch McCaslin, J. D. McCaslin**, and **Joe Galini** for their example, encouragement, friendship, and their introduction to Herschel Sanders.
- **Larry Cantrell, Guy Owen, L. M. Cummings, Clyde Hensley, Tracy Wood, Merle Fraser, Ben Thomas, Mark Huey, Joe Galindo**, and **Robin Blakeley** for their encouragement and support.
- **Kathy Jones** for her prayers and her faithful service in operating, supporting, and maintaining *Koenig's International News*.
- **Robert Durand** for his invaluable writing, editing, and formatting assistance with our commentaries at the web site each week.
- **Joan Koenig**, my mother, **Virg Koenig**, my father, **Ted Koenig**, my brother, for their love and encouragement.
- **Ruth Scofield** (Prince of Peace Embassy in Washington) for her love of the Lord and her introduction to Pearl McLane.
- **Pearl McLane** (Dove of Life Ministries) for the opportunity to experience her passion for and knowledge of Scripture and for her introduction to John McTernan.
- **Patti May** for her encouragement, prayers, and support.
- our loyal contributors who have helped to make this important news ministry possible.
- those who have lifted their prayers for the Lord's blessing on the work we do in His service.
- and last, but certainly not least, **John McTernan** for his love of the Bible and his sensitivity to those things that matter to the Lord, helping us all to become much more effective watchmen.

Table of Contents

The Blessing and the Curse

And it shall come to pass, when all these things are come
upon thee, the blessing and the curse, which I have set
before thee, and thou shalt call them to mind among all
the nations, whither the Lord thy God hath driven
thee. . . .

—Deuteronomy 30:1

On May 13, 1948, General George Marshall wired David
Ben-Gurion that if he declared an independent nation of Israel, five Arab armies would march, and within
forty-eight hours not one Jew in the land would be left alive.
The rest is history.

In the wake of the 1948 Jewish war for independence,
most of the free world, including the United States, welcomed the new state of Israel. Finally, after two thousand
years, the wandering Jew could have a safe place to rest
his weary feet. No longer would the Jews have to fear such
massacres as the Hitler Holocaust in which over six million Jews, including over a million children, were extermi-
nated. Yet, more than five decades later, there is no peace
in Jerusalem. Every Israeli boy and girl has to serve in the
army to protect the citizens of Israel from wars and inter-
nal terrorist activity. In every Jewish home there is fear
and concern for the future. The mindset of the Arab world
is that it can lose ninety-nine wars; all they have to do is to

win the one hundredth war.

After leading some forty tours to Israel, the number one tourist destination in the world, my last one in June 2001 was one of the very few in the country. The sites and hotels were practically empty. Tourists from America, Europe, Japan, and other nations were traveling abroad, but practically none were going to Israel. Why? Fear! The U.S. State Department had signaled Israel as the number one most dangerous place on earth.

On June 25, 2001, Rani Levy, special advisor to Prime Minister Sharon of Israel, spoke to my tour group in Jerusalem. Within the context of his address, he stated, "No person, no nation, no international forum, can bring peace to this land. Peace can only come with Divine intervention and the coming of Messiah."

Josephus records that in the final days of the Roman siege of Jerusalem in A.D. 70, the priests would go throughout the city encouraging the Jews to hold out, because the Messiah was coming. The Messiah did not come, because the people rejected the Messiah. Peter and John had preached to Israel that if the people and rulers would understand that Jesus was the Messiah, and cry out to God to send Him back, He would have come back at that time (Acts 3:11–26).

The prophetic scenario for the dispersion of Israel into all the world after A.D. 70, their extreme persecution in the nations of the world, their return, and their ultimate blessings in the Kingdom age, were recorded by Hosea:

> For the children of Israel shall abide many days without a king, and without a prince, and without a sacrifice, and without an image. . . . Afterward shall the children of Israel return, and seek the Lord their God, and David their king; and shall fear the Lord and his goodness in

the latter days. . . . I will go and return to my place, till they acknowledge their offence, and seek my face: in their affliction [tribulation] they will seek me early. Come, and let us return unto the Lord: for he hath torn, and he will heal us; he hath smitten, and he will bind us up. After two days will he revive us: in the third day he will raise us up, and we shall live in his sight.

—Hosea 3:4–5; 5:15; 6:1–2

An entire dissertation could be written on these few verses alone, but the main point we wish to address is that the prophet was obviously not referencing two twenty-four–hour days. God's ratio in time of one day to a thousand years is set forth in Psalm 90 and Second Peter 3. Israel has been scattered into the world without a Temple or a sacrifice, smitten and torn, for two thousand years. I believe the people of Israel are seeking the Lord today. Evangelical Christians believe the Messiah for whom they are seeking is the Lord Jesus Christ who is coming again; religious Jews as yet do not know the identity of their coming Messiah. As Dr. Maurice Jaffe, former head rabbi of the Great Synagogue, and president of the Association of Israeli Synagogue, used to say to me, "You believe that Jesus is our Messiah, but we Jews are willing to wait and see who he will be."

A better day is coming for Israel: "The stone which the builders refused is become the head stone of the corner. This is the Lord's doing; it is marvellous in our eyes. This is the day which the Lord hath made; we will rejoice and be glad in it. . . . Blessed be he that cometh in the name of the Lord . . ." (Psalm 118:22–26). "Behold, your house is left unto you desolate. For I say unto you, Ye shall not see me henceforth, till ye shall say, Blessed is he that cometh in the name of the Lord" (Matthew 23:38–39).

Down through the Christian era, segments of the church
have mistakenly persecuted the Jews, thinking they are doing God's service. It is no wonder today that many Israelis
are still skeptical in regard to Christian affiliations. Yet, today evangelical Christians are the best friends that Israel
has in the world. God has made tremendous and exciting
covenants and promises to Israel that will be fulfilled. "I
say then, Hath God cast away his people? God forbid. For I
also am an Israelite. . . . God hath not cast away his people
which he foreknew . . ." (Romans 11:1–2).

As Moses prophesied, the nation of Israel in its history
has experienced both the blessings of God and the curse of
God when they forgot Him and His covenants. But there is
also a blessing for Gentiles who bless Israel and a curse
from God upon Gentiles who bring harm to Israel or the
Jews: "And I will bless them that bless thee, and curse him
that curseth thee: and in thee shall all families of the earth
be blessed" (Genesis 12:3).

History records that no nation or race has ever persecuted Israel or the Jews and escaped the wrath of God.
That Israel has deserved its own punishment is prophetically declared by the prophets, but it is God Himself that
brings judgment to His earthly people, not others. The more
our nation blesses Israel, the more God will bless us. However, as John McTernan and Bill Koenig document in this
book, in recent years when our government for political or
material advantage has conspired with Israel's enemies,
God has given us severe warnings.

As Christians, we are to keep the peace of Jerusalem in
our prayers, for when we pray for peace in Jerusalem, we
are actually praying for the Lord to return; because, there
can be no peace in the Holy City until He reigns on Mt.
Zion.

—Dr. N. W. Hutchings

Preface

In *Israel: The Blessing or the Curse,* you will read about the nation of Israel and the impact that this small Middle East nation is having on the world's peace. What is happening these days is truly remarkable. But then again, we shouldn't be surprised, because the Old Testament prophet Zechariah prewarned us about these events many years ago:

> And in that day will I make Jerusalem a burdensome stone for all people: all that burden themselves with it shall be cut in pieces, though all the people of the earth be gathered together against it. . . . And it shall come to pass in that day, that I will seek to destroy all the nations that come against Jerusalem.
>
> —Zechariah 12:3,9

In reflection, over the last ten years many major world figures have been involved in the Middle East peace process pertaining to Israel's land. These are some of the most influential political and business leaders in the world. They have all pushed Israel to give up God's covenant land. Their influence has even persuaded the Israeli government to participate in the "land for peace" scheme.

Israel is not to give up her covenant land; the land was a gift from God to Abraham and his descendants through the Abrahamic covenant. However, the leaders of modern-day Israel hoped that the "land for peace" plan would work. It has greatly failed, and this nation—the "apple of God's eye" is now at the most dangerous point in her history.

Today, the Muslim nations who have persuaded the world powers to help in the "land for peace" plan are closing in on Israel. They have brought her to the edge of war. However, the Bible says that God will be Israel's protector. The Scriptures indicate that the world will side with the Arab nations and that God will stand with Israel. In Zechariah 12:9, the Bible also says clearly that those who come against Israel will be destroyed.

From May 6 to August 31, 2001, many nations, political organizations, and church organizations throughout the world have publicly stated their positions regarding Israel's land. That list includes many churches who believe that they have replaced Israel in significance, rather than being grafted in with the Jews (Romans 11:11–24). Even the Vatican, representing 900 million Roman Catholic followers, has signed an agreement with the Palestinians, who represent 1.2 billion Muslims, about the future of Jerusalem. They are attempting to force Israel to share Jerusalem, but in essence they are publicly coming against the covenant land of Israel. The promise of Zechariah 12:9 also applies to the Vatican.

As these words are being written, the only nation that continues to stand with Israel is the U.S. Ironically, the U.S. has also been the sponsor of the "land for peace" plans that have put the nation of Israel at the brink of war. The U.S. sponsored the Madrid, Oslo, Wye, Tenet, and Mitchell plans. These plans are all contrary to the Word of God.

We have a very fair and loving God. He has allowed the Middle East peace process to play out for ten years on the world stage. He is now allowing the organizations and nations of the world to express their positions publicly pertaining to Israel.

The September 11, 2001, events in New York and Washington, the "911 National Day of Emergency," was America's wake-up call. The Lord has said, "enough is enough." Over and over again in the past five years, many near tragedies have been avoided. There is no doubt that the restraining hand of the Lord has kept these situations from being much worse. This time, it wasn't stopped. We have seen close calls over the years, but September 11, 2001, was a direct hit. The Lord is tired of being mocked, of seeing the shedding of innocent blood, of being confronted with the gay agenda, the materialism, and the debauchery in the United States.

The World Trade Center and Pentagon terrorist events have also allowed the world to see and learn about radical Islam. Many Americans now have a better idea of what Israel is faced with daily.

The authors are in no way making direct personal attacks on any one person in this book. The important point to remember is that the men and women named herein have and will be used by the Lord to bring world events to a very crucial stage. Whether their plans were honorable or diabolic, these people were not immune from God's directive pertaining to the covenant land of Israel. In other words, don't come against the "apple of God's eye," and don't touch Israel's covenant land, or you will pay the price.

The Lord has prewarned, in clear detail to be found in His Word, anyone with ears to hear or eyes to see what lies ahead. And now, events are playing out exactly the way He prophesied through the Old Testament prophets and the words of His Son Jesus Christ in the Gospels. These are the most exciting times in human history.

We hope you enjoy and become more informed by our work. We serve an awesome God, and we are humbled by this opportunity to bring you this information, because our only hope is in Jesus Christ. "And now, Lord, what wait I for? my hope is in thee" (Psalm 39:7).

Chapter 1

Is the Bible the Word of God?

The grass withereth, the flower fadeth: but the word of
our God shall stand for ever.

—Isaiah 40:8

For ever, O LORD, thy word is settled in heaven.

—Psalm 119:89

But my words and my statutes, which I commanded my
servants the prophets.

—Zechariah 1:6

Through the years, I have spoken to many people about
God and the Bible. On a number of occasions, the question was posed, What proof is there of God? A similar question asked is, How do you know the Bible is the Word of God? There are many ways to answer this question, but I have taken the approach that the authority of the Bible being God's Word can be seen through the Jew and the nation of Israel.

The understanding for why God called the nation of Israel; the history of the nation; and the prophecy related to Israel, will show the awesome authority of the Bible as the Word of God. If Israel is understood spiritually and not just politically, an entirely new and exciting reality of the time we live in unravels. We are now living in the time that the ancient Jewish prophets wrote about. The nation of Israel has been reborn and Jerusalem is once again the capital of the Jewish nation. The reality of God and the Bible then can be "proved" through the fulfillment of what the Bible states about the nation of Israel. What an awesome concept this is—Bible prophecy is alive before our very eyes. The rebirth of the nation of Israel in our day is unique among all the nations in history. The entire nation was destroyed twice, but both times it came back into existence. Not only was the nation destroyed twice, but each time nearly all the people were taken captive into foreign countries. Yet, they returned to the land. All this points to the uniqueness of Israel, that it is not a nation like other nations.

In 586 B.C., the great Babylonian king Nebuchadnezzar destroyed the nation, Jerusalem, and the Temple. This destruction resulted in nearly all the Jews being taken captive to Babylon. The Jews remained in Babylon for seventy years and then returned to rebuild Jerusalem and their Temple. The Romans, some six hundred fifty years later in A.D. 70, again destroyed the nation, Jerusalem, and the Temple. The Jews were scattered into the nations. In 136 A.D. the Jews again revolted against Rome. The Jews were once again totally defeated and they were dispersed into all the world. Very few Jews remained on the land after this war with Rome. The devastation was awesome.

Israel should have ended as a nation and probably as a people in 586 B.C., but it survived. Israel, definitely should have ended as a nation in A.D. 70, but as the ancient Bible prophets wrote, the nation was literally reborn. After ceasing to be a nation for almost nineteen hundred years, on May 14, 1948, Israel was once again a nation. This was followed in June 1967 with a united Jerusalem once again the capital. The Hebrew language had become almost extinct, but yet today the Israelis speak Hebrew. They speak the same language as their ancestors. They kept the same religion while in exile. There is simply no nation like Israel.

Several years ago, I took a tour of the biblical sites in Israel. The tour stopped at the museum of the Dead Sea Scrolls. In the center of the building was a circular glass cabinet. This cabinet was huge in its length, and the entire Isaiah scroll was opened in it. The scroll was set in the cabinet and lighted so it could be read. I asked the Israeli tour guide if he could read the scroll. He went to the scroll and started to read a two thousand-year-old document written in ancient Hebrew. He said it was somewhat hard to read because the letters where shaped a little differently than modern Hebrew. As he started to read, I realized it was Isaiah 59. I had him read back in the scroll until he found Isaiah 53 (the Bible was not divided into chapters until the 1500s). This chapter is one of my favorites in the Bible. To my amazement, he read this chapter to me.

A language which was nearly extinct was read to me by a man whose nation had been destroyed nineteen hundred years ago! There was no English language two thousand years ago. It is very difficult to read English from only two hundred years ago. What other nation is like Israel?

The Covenant with Abraham

The key to understanding the modern nation of Israel is the covenant God made with Abraham thousands of years ago. Abraham is one of the key figures in the Bible. In fact, Abraham is referred to as the friend of God. God told Abraham that whoever blessed him would be blessed and whoever cursed him would be cursed, and through Abraham all the families of the earth would be blessed (Genesis 12:3). **So, when dealing with Abraham there is a blessing or a curse.** It is imperative that both individuals and nations deal with Abraham and his descendants according to God's Word.

The Bible records that God made an everlasting covenant with Abraham and his descendants. This covenant involved the land of Canaan which today is the nation of Israel. The land given by God to Abraham was from the Mediterranean Sea on the west to the Euphrates River on the east. On the north, the land included all of modern Lebanon and most of Syria to Egypt on the south. The land promised to Abraham and his seed is found in Genesis. "In the same day the LORD made a covenant with Abram, saying, Unto thy seed have I given this land, from the river of Egypt unto the great river, the river Euphrates" (Genesis 15:18).

After Moses died and the children of Israel were about to enter the promised land, Joshua was given a very specific description of the land grant that God had given Abraham, Isaac, and Jacob. God again confirmed the everlasting covenant, this time with Joshua. The children of Israel moved into the land under this description of the area given to them by God.

> Moses my servant is dead; now therefore arise, go over this Jordan, thou, and all this people, unto the land which I do give to them, even to the children of Israel. . . . From the wilderness and this Lebanon even unto the great river, the river Euphrates, all the land of the Hittites, and unto the great sea toward the going down of the sun, shall be your coast.
>
> —Joshua 1:2, 4

Today the idea of entering into a covenant is really not used too often; however, a covenant between two parties is a very serious matter. The *Merriam-Webster Dictionary* defines a covenant as: *1. a usual formal, solemn, and binding agreement, compact; 2. a written agreement or promise usually*

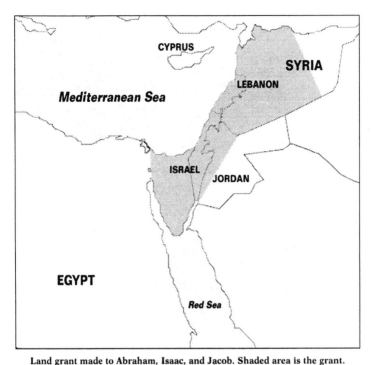

Land grant made to Abraham, Isaac, and Jacob. Shaded area is the grant.

under seal between two parties especially for the performance of some action. God then made a binding agreement with Abraham that the land of Israel would belong to Abraham forever. The performance on God's part was to see that the land would be Abraham's forever. Abraham was not required to do anything but to believe God. The everlasting covenant God made with Abraham follows:

> And I will establish my covenant between me and thee and thy seed after thee in their generations for an **everlasting covenant**, to be a God unto thee, and to thy seed after thee. And I will give unto thee, and to thy seed after thee, the land wherein thou art a stranger, all the land of Canaan, for an **everlasting possession**; and I will be their God.
>
> —Genesis 17:7–8

Abraham had two sons, Ishmael and Isaac. Ishmael was the oldest, but God bypassed Ishmael and renewed the covenant with Isaac. God made the same covenant with Isaac over the land of Israel that He had made with Abraham. When God renewed the covenant through Isaac, He also made it with Isaac's descendants. The renewing of the covenant with Isaac is found in Genesis chapter 26.

> Sojourn in this land, and I will be with thee, and will bless thee; for unto thee, and unto thy seed, I will give all these countries, and I will perform the oath which I sware unto Abraham thy father; And I will make thy seed to multiply as the stars of heaven, and will give unto thy seed all these countries; and in thy seed shall all the nations of the earth be blessed;
>
> —Genesis 26:3–4

God then renewed the covenant with Abraham's grandson Jacob. This covenant was the same as with Abraham and Isaac, and it was going to be with their descendants. God had established a definite genealogy through which this covenant was going to follow.

> And God said unto him, I am God Almighty: be fruitful and multiply; a nation and a company of nations shall be of thee, and kings shall come out of thy loins; And the land which I gave Abraham and Isaac, to thee I will give it, and to thy seed after thee will I give the land.
>
> —Genesis 35:11–12

God's Chosen People

Sometimes the expression is used that the Jews are "God's chosen people." Upon being questioned, very few people know why the Jews are referred to as "God's chosen people." God made the covenant with Abraham and his descendants for a reason. God wanted to reveal Himself, and He chose Abraham and his descendants as His vehicle. God has several reasons for making the covenant with Abraham. He wanted a people to bring forth the prophets and give the world the Bible (Romans 3:2). The nation was to be a light to the surrounding pagans (Isaiah 43:12). The Messiah would come from the descendants of Abraham (Isaiah 9:6–7), and the land would be the place where the Messiah would be born (Micah 5:2). God has clearly linked His name with Israel. The authority of the Bible as God's Word can be put to the test through this everlasting covenant. God made this covenant with Abraham and his descendants so the people of the earth could see the authority of God's Word.

> The LORD shall establish thee an holy people unto himself, as he hath sworn unto thee, if thou shalt keep the commandments of the LORD thy God, and walk in his ways. And all people of the earth shall see that thou art called by the name of the LORD; and they shall be afraid of thee.
>
> —Deuteronomy 28:9 –10

The name of God was now directly linked to the nation of Israel: "And they shall put my name upon the children of Israel; and I will bless them" (Numbers 6:27).

About five hundred years after Abraham, God made a second covenant. This covenant had to do with the giving of the law to Moses. The law which reflected God's holiness was given to the children of Israel. This covenant was conditional and based upon the requirements of the law being met by the nation. "Now therefore, if ye will obey my voice indeed, and keep my covenant, then ye shall be a peculiar treasure unto me above all people: for all the earth is mine" (Exodus 19:5).

If God's law was obeyed, the Jews would be blessed above all people; however, if they disobeyed they would be punished. One of the punishments would be the destruction of the nation and the dispersion of the people into all the countries. Either way, the authority of God's Word could be seen through Israel being blessed above all nations or being cursed and dispersed into the world. Israel now reflected God's holy name. God now had a people that the entire world could see His awesome power working through. God's plan for the redemption of mankind was directly tied to the descendants of Abraham.

In the second covenant, the blessings or the curses depended on the nation of Israel. God warned that if the people disobeyed His covenant they would be driven off the land and into the nations. The destruction of the nation would be because of sin and rebellion against God's Word. Israel did break the covenant, and exactly as God had warned, the nation was destroyed and the people driven into all the countries of the world. God sent prophet after prophet to warn Israel of the coming judgment. Israel rejected the message of the prophets and based on the second covenant, the nation was destroyed. God kept His covenant. The first destruction lasted seventy years, while the second was for nineteen hundred years.

The following are some of the scriptures which warn Israel of the dispersion into the nations:

+ Deuteronomy 28:64: "And the LORD shall scatter thee among all people, from the one end of the earth even unto the other; and there thou shalt serve other gods, which neither thou nor thy fathers have known, even wood and stone."
+ Deuteronomy 30:1: "And it shall come to pass, when all these things are come upon thee, the blessing and

the curse, which I have set before thee, and thou shalt call them to mind among all the nations, whither the LORD thy God hath driven thee."

♦ Leviticus 26:32–33: "And I will bring the land into desolation: and your enemies which dwell therein shall be astonished at it. And I will scatter you among the heathen, and will draw out a sword after you: and your land shall be desolate, and your cities waste."

The Bible and history record that Israel failed to keep the requirements of the second covenant and was cast into the nations. In 70 A.D., the Roman army destroyed Israel, Jerusalem, and the Temple. This began the great dispersion of Israel into all the nations of the world. God fulfilled His covenant with Israel to the very letter. The dispersion of the Jews was an awesome witness to the authority of God's Word, the Bible. However, the dispersion is only half the covenant. God promised to restore the people back to the land and literally have the nation of Israel reborn. The awesome power of God in ruling over the affairs of the nations can be seen in the history of the nation of Israel.

When looking at the Bible about the history of Israel, one must understand that the Jews are no different than any other people when it comes to sin. Without understanding the human heart, it could be very easy to condemn Israel for failing God and rebelling against Him. If God had chosen any other people to work through, the result would have been the same. The sin nature is the same in the Jew as in others. Any other people would have also failed. The sin nature is the same in all people. The prophet Jeremiah states about the sin nature, "The heart is deceitful above all things, and desperately wicked: who can know it?" (Jeremiah 17:9).

When God made the unconditional covenant with Abraham, He did not depend on man to uphold it. The unconditional covenant freed God from depending on the weakness of man's nature to fulfill it. No matter if Israel failed, God could still work His will because of the everlasting covenant.

Although Israel was to break the covenant, God said that He would never completely reject the nation and He would always honor the everlasting covenant with Abraham, Isaac, and Jacob. Because of this everlasting covenant, He would one day restore the nation of Israel and bring the people back into the land. The destruction of Israel and the restoration of the nation is an awesome witness to the authority of the Bible as the Word of God. The Bible can literally be tested as the very Word of God with the covenant God made with Abraham and his descendants. The nation of Israel then becomes one of the main focal points with God because His name is linked by covenant with it.

The Bible with great clarity states that Israel would one day be reborn, and this would happen because of the everlasting covenant with Abraham. Let us look at some of these verses:

Then will I remember my covenant with Jacob, and also my covenant with Isaac, and also my covenant with Abraham will I remember; and I will remember the land. The land also shall be left of them, and shall enjoy her sabbaths, while she lieth desolate without them: and they shall accept of the punishment of their iniquity: because, even because they despised my judgments, and because their soul abhorred my statutes. And yet for all that, when they be in the land of their enemies, I will not cast them away, neither will I abhor them, to destroy them utterly, and to break my covenant with them: for I am the LORD their God. But I will for their sakes remember the covenant of their ancestors, whom I brought forth out of the land of Egypt in the sight of the heathen, that I might be their God: I am the LORD.

—Leviticus 26:42–45

The idea of the Jews returning to the covenant land was promised over and over again by Moses. There was no mistaking that there would be a worldwide dispersion followed by a total restoration. Moses did not give the time gap between the dispersion and restoration.

That then the LORD thy God will turn thy captivity, and have compassion upon thee, and will return and gather thee from all the nations, whither the LORD thy God hath scattered thee. If any of thine be driven out unto the outmost parts of heaven, from thence will the LORD thy God gather thee, and from thence will he fetch thee: And the LORD thy God will bring thee into the land which thy fathers possessed, and thou shalt possess it; and he will do thee good, and multiply thee above thy fathers.

—Deuteronomy 30:3–5

The Ancient Prophets Speak to Us Today

Prophet after prophet in the Bible tell of the restoration of Israel after being dispersed into all the world. God sent prophets to Israel to warn them of the coming judgment on the nation. The prophets warned of the destruction of the nation based on the second covenant. But, these same prophets also comforted the Jewish people by telling them the nation would be restored. The prophets also spoke of the coming of the Messiah and the golden age of His rule on earth. But, before the rule of the Messiah, the nation had to be restored.

There are several themes of prophecy in the Bible. These themes include the coming of the Messiah, the day of the Lord, the messianic age, and heaven and hell. The theme of the dispersion and restoration of the nation of Israel is one of the major focuses in the Bible. There is verse after verse in the Bible about the rebirth of Israel. The prophets Ezekiel and Zechariah devote entire chapters to this theme. The prophecy about the rebirth of Israel from a worldwide dispersion is not a footnote in the Bible. This theme is written on page after page by prophet after prophet for all to clearly see.

When the prophets spoke about the rebirth of Israel, it was based on the everlasting covenant with Abraham and the promises made in the second covenant with Moses. The message of the prophets was not new. These messages were given to comfort the children of Israel and warn the world that the covenant with Abraham was still in effect. The Jewish people were dispersed under the second covenant, but one day would be brought back into the land under the everlasting covenant. Let us look at what these ancient prophets wrote that has such a clear message for today.

Isaiah

The prophet Isaiah about 750 B.C. wrote about the rebirth of Israel from a worldwide dispersion. About one hundred fifty years after Isaiah, the nation was destroyed and the people were taken captive to Babylon. This was the first dispersion. After seventy years in captivity, some returned and rebuilt the country, Jerusalem, and the Temple. This was not a worldwide dispersion. Isaiah was writing about the rebirth of the nation from a worldwide dispersion. This has happened in our life time. The worldwide dispersion was the second. The Jews have now come back to Israel literally from the east, west, north, and south. To the location of Jerusalem, they have returned from the ends of the earth.

- Isaiah 11:11–12: "And it shall come to pass in that day, that the Lord shall set his hand again the second time to recover the remnant of his people, which shall be left, from Assyria, and from Egypt, and from Pathros, and from Cush, and from Elam, and from Shinar, and from Hamath, and from the islands of the sea. And he shall set up an ensign for the nations, and shall assemble the outcasts of Israel, and gather together the dispersed of Judah from the four corners of the earth."

- Isaiah 43:5–6: "Fear not: for I am with thee: I will bring thy seed from the east, and gather thee from the west; I will say to the north, Give up; and to the south, Keep not back: bring my sons from far, and my daughters from the ends of the earth."

Jeremiah

Jeremiah was a prophet right at the time of the first dispersion. This was about 600 B.C. He warned the people of the coming captivity in Babylon, but he also warned about another dispersion into all the world. He prophesied that the people would return from the coming captivity to Babylon and also from a worldwide captivity. The prophets all warned of the coming judgment, but they also comforted Israel that there would be a restoration. Jeremiah like all the prophets told of the rebirth of the nation. Jeremiah states that the return of the Jews was going to be the direct act of God. God was going to be directly involved in leading the Jews back to Israel. This regathering of the people was to be a warning to the nations. Remember, these verses were written twenty-six hundred years ago.

Behold, I will bring them from the north country, and gather them from the coasts of the earth, and with them the blind and the lame, the woman with child and her that travaileth with child together: a great company shall return thither. They shall come with weeping, and with supplications will I lead them: I will cause them to walk by the rivers of waters in a straight way, wherein they shall not stumble: for I am a father to Israel, and Ephraim is my firstborn. Hear the word of the LORD, O ye nations, and declare it in the isles afar off, and say, He that scattered Israel will gather him, and keep him, as a shepherd doth his flock.

—Jeremiah 31:8–10

Jeremiah said the rebirth of the nation would be greater than the exodus from Egypt under Moses. The Jews coming back to Israel from the nations of the world would surpass the exodus from Egypt. This regathering would be of such a magnitude that no longer would the exodus have such a great impact, but the worldwide regathering would supplant it. This regathering would be based on the covenant that was made with their ancestors.

Therefore, behold, the days come, saith the LORD, that it shall no more be said, The LORD liveth, that brought up the children of Israel out of the land of Egypt; But, The LORD liveth, that brought up the children of Israel from the land of the north, and from all the lands whither he had driven them: and I will bring them again into their land that I gave unto their fathers.

—Jeremiah 16:14–15

Ezekiel
The prophet Ezekiel lived and wrote during the first exile,

about 570 B.C. He was taken captive by King Nebuchadnezzar and brought to Babylon. While in Babylon, Ezekiel
wrote incredibly detailed prophecies about the worldwide
dispersion and rebirth of the nation of Israel. In beautifully
written language with awesome imagery, the prophet gives
a detailed look of God's plan for Israel and the nations.
Entire chapters of Ezekiel are devoted to the dispersion,
restoration, and events that happen after the restoration.

Chapter thirty-six gives a panoramic view of what was
going to happen to Israel. This chapter first talks about the
nation being destroyed and the land wasted. He follows
with the promise the land will once again be fruitful and
inhabited. Ezekiel promises they would again dwell in the
land that God promised to their fathers. The fathers would
be Abraham, Isaac, and Jacob with whom God made the
everlasting covenant. Ezekiel ties the regathering of Jews
from all the nations with the everlasting covenant.

> And I scattered them among the heathen, and they were
> dispersed through the countries: according to their way
> and according to their doings I judged them. . . . For I
> will take you from among the heathen, and gather you
> out of all countries, and will bring you into your own
> land. . . . And ye shall dwell in the land that I gave to
> your fathers; and ye shall be my people, and I will be
> your God.
> —Ezekiel 36:19, 24, 28

Ezekiel follows the general statements in chapter thirty-six
about the regathering of the nation with a vivid picture in
chapter thirty-seven. With some of the most graphic imagery in the entire Bible, Ezekiel describes the rebirth of the
nation of Israel. The nation was described as being a huge
pile of dead, dried bones lying in a valley. In reading this
chapter, the picture comes to mind of the prophet standing

on a mountain ledge over looking a large valley full of dead men's dry bones. One can almost see the noonday sun shining on these bones causing them to glisten white. God gives this picture to show the utter hopelessness of the nation of Israel. The nation was completely dead with no hope of ever living. What hope can dead men's bones have for ever living again, none!

To the natural eye, Israel had no hope. The nation was destroyed. The people dispersed into all the world. The language was gone, and they were persecuted and rejected from country to country. The vision of the valley of the dead bones was a perfect picture of the nation of Israel after its destruction in A.D. 70. There was no hope. But, Ezekiel does not end with the hopelessness. He shows that by a sovereign act of God, the nation will be reborn. God is going to work in the affairs of men and governments to resurrect the valley of dried bones into an exceedingly great army. This will happen according to the will of God to fulfill His covenant.

Let us look at the picture Ezekiel gives of the hope of the nation of Israel being reborn.

> The hand of the LORD was upon me, and carried me out in the spirit of the LORD, and set me down in the midst of the valley which was full of bones, And caused me to pass by them round about: and, behold, there were very many in the open valley; and, lo, they were very dry. And he said unto me, Son of man, can these bones live? And I answered, O Lord GOD, thou knowest. Again he said unto me, Prophesy upon these bones, and say unto them, O ye dry bones, hear the word of the LORD. Thus saith the Lord GOD unto these bones; Behold, I will cause breath to enter into you, and ye shall live: And I will lay sinews upon you, and will bring up flesh upon you, and

cover you with skin, and put breath in you, and ye shall live; and ye shall know that I am the LORD. So I prophesied as I was commanded: and as I prophesied, there was a noise, and behold a shaking, and the bones came together, bone to his bone. And when I beheld, lo, the sinews and the flesh came up upon them, and the skin covered them above: but there was no breath in them. Then said he unto me, Prophesy unto the wind, prophesy, son of man, and say to the wind, Thus saith the Lord GOD; Come from the four winds, O breath, and breathe upon these slain, that they may live. So I prophesied as he commanded me, and the breath came into them, and they lived, and stood up upon their feet, an exceeding great army.

—Ezekiel 37:1–10

Immediately, after giving this powerful imagery of the nation, Ezekiel then goes on to explain the vision. There can be no doubt whatsoever the theme of this vision. The bones are the people of Israel without hope, and they are dead in the nations. The prophet calls the nations of the world Israel's graves. The coming together of the bones into a body is the nation being reborn.

Then he said unto me, Son of man, these bones are the whole house of Israel: behold, they say, Our bones are dried, and our hope is lost: we are cut off for our parts. Therefore prophesy and say unto them, Thus saith the Lord GOD; Behold, O my people, I will open your graves, and cause you to come up out of your graves, and bring you into the land of Israel. . . . And say unto them, Thus saith the Lord GOD; Behold, I will take the children of Israel from among the heathen, whither they be gone, and will gather them on every side, and bring them into

their own land: . . . And they shall dwell in the land that
I have given unto Jacob my servant, wherein your fathers have dwelt; and they shall dwell therein, even they,
and their children, and their children's children for ever.
—Ezekiel 37:11–12, 21, 25

Ezekiel connects the resurrection of the nation from the
dead, with the land being given to Jacob. This is again a
reference to the covenant. Time after time, over and over
again, the Bible connects the dispersion and rebirth of Israel with the everlasting covenant. When the nation is reborn the Bible is crystal clear, it will be because of God
honoring His covenant. God is working in the affairs of
men and nations to fulfill His ancient promise. God cannot
lie. God's word cannot fail.

Zechariah

Zechariah was one of the prophets after the Jews returned
to Israel from the Babylonian captivity. He wrote about 520
B.C. Zechariah is unique in that so much of his focus is on
the city of Jerusalem. The other prophets talk about the
land and some touch upon Jerusalem, but Zechariah gives
details about the city. The prophet says that God has chosen Jerusalem for His purpose. Of all the cities of the world,
God has chosen the city of Jerusalem to work out His redemption plan for man. "And the LORD shall inherit Judah
his portion in the holy land, and shall choose Jerusalem
again" (Zechariah 2:12).

Zechariah shows that Jerusalem, just like Israel, would
be inhabited and restored. The people would come back to
Jerusalem from all over the world. "Thus saith the LORD of
hosts; Behold, I will save my people from the east country,
and from the west country; And I will bring them, and they
shall dwell in the midst of Jerusalem: and they shall be my

people, and I will be their God, in truth and in righteousness" (Zechariah 8:7–8).

The city will be the center for the worship of God. All the peoples from the nations of the world would come to Jerusalem. The city would be the center of world attention. Jerusalem is unlike any city in the world because it is the city God has chosen. This city will be once again the capital of a reborn nation of Israel. "Yea, many people and strong nations shall come to seek the LORD of hosts in Jerusalem, and to pray before the LORD" (Zechariah 8:22). ". . . And Jerusalem shall be inhabited again in her own place, even in Jerusalem" (Zechariah 12:6).

When the Jews returned from their worldwide dispersion and the nation was reborn, it would be the final return. There will be no second or third dispersion into all the world. For this reason, the events that are unfolding before our very eyes are so significant. God is working in the affairs of the nations to bring what was written in the Bible to a conclusion. Remember, when the Jews returned from the worldwide dispersion, it would be final. The world is now entering into the end play of God's prophetic plan for our age. The entire script has already been written by the prophets. It is there for everyone to read, understand and believe. Remember, this is the final rebirth of the nation of Israel. "But Judah shall dwell for ever, and Jerusalem from generation to generation" (Joel 3:20).

Chapter 2

Times of the Gentiles

The covenant that God made with Abraham, Isaac, and Jacob cannot fail. It is based upon God upholding His everlasting promise and not the Jews keeping it. Israel was twice destroyed and now twice restored. There is no other nation in history like this. How else can the survival of the Jews be understood except by this covenant with God?

The nation of Israel was reborn just as the Bible said it would happen. We are now living in the times the ancient Jewish prophets wrote about. The prophecy about Israel does not stop with the rebirth of the nation. The Bible has laid out the future. As time goes on, God's prophetic plan as outlined in the Bible has become clearer and clearer. The nation of Israel and Jerusalem in particular are God's time piece. By watching events involving Israel and Jerusalem, the prophetic time can be determined. Jesus Christ said that Jerusalem was God's prophetic time piece. He said that Jerusalem would be trodden down by non-Jews (Gentiles) until a certain fixed period of time. This fixed period of time had to do with the end of the age and His second coming. "And they shall fall by the edge of the sword, and shall be led away captive into all nations: and Jerusalem shall be trodden down of the Gentiles, until the times of the Gentiles be fulfilled" (Luke 21:24).

The times of the Gentiles began in 606 B.C. when King Nebuchadnezzar first conquered Jerusalem. In 586 B.C., he destroyed Jerusalem and led the Jews captive to Babylon. He ended the rule of the kings of Israel. From 586 B.C. onward, Israel never had another king. The nation was at the mercy of one empire after another. The Babylonian, Persian, Greek, and Roman empires all ruled over Jerusalem. The entire time the Jews were still under the covenant with God.

In A.D. 66, the Jews revolted against Rome. This resulted in the total destruction of Jerusalem with over one million being killed. In A.D. 70, the Roman general Titus destroyed Israel and Jerusalem. The Temple was destroyed which ended the priesthood and sacrificial system. Many of the survivors of this war were sold as slaves.

In 136, a second Jewish revolt against Rome was crushed. Jerusalem was literally plowed up by the Romans and the soil salted to poison it. The Roman emperor Hadrian renamed Jerusalem, calling it Aelia Capitolina. The remaining Jews were sold as slaves. Very few Jews remained on the covenant land. The nation of Israel was literally dead until 1948. For almost nineteen hundred years, there was no Israel. On May 14, 1948, through United Nations action, Israel once again became a nation. On this day, David Ben-Gurion, the first prime minister of the modern state of Israel proclaimed the state back into existence.

God used the Babylonians and Romans to fulfill His covenant with Israel. These pagan nations could only have authority over God's covenant people because the Jews failed to keep the law. The Babylonians took away the kingdom and the Romans the priesthood. They were God's instruments of judgment. The everlasting covenant with Abraham still stood through these judgments. Even though the Romans completely destroyed the nation, the covenant was still in effect to bring the Jews back into the land. The duration of the destruction was not mentioned in the Bible, but the promise of the covenant remained.

The prophet Hosea writing about 750 B.c., said that Israel would suffer a long time without a king and priesthood, but in the latter days they would return to the land. At the end of the age, the Jews would return to the land which would be followed by a return to God and the Messiah. They have returned in our lifetime. "For the children of Israel shall abide many days without a king, and without a prince, and without a sacrifice. . . . Afterward shall the children of Israel return, and seek the LORD their God, and David their king; and shall fear the LORD and his goodness in the latter days" (Hosea 3:4–5).

The expression, seeking David their king, means seeking the Messiah. David was dead two hundred years when Hosea wrote. The Messiah was to be a direct descendant of David. He was to be the son of David and King over all the earth. The prophet Jeremiah told of a captivity into Babylon that was to last for seventy years. This captivity did not destroy the priesthood. When the Jews returned after seventy years, they immediately restored the sacrificial system and rebuilt the Temple. The captivity Hosea wrote about was for a very long time in which there would be no sacrificial system. This destruction of the priesthood began in the year 70 and continues to this day.

The destruction of the Jewish Temple in Jerusalem by the Romans ties directly with the destruction of the Temple by the Babylonians. This connection is amazing. Both Temples where destroyed on the very same day, only six hundred fifty-five years apart. In 586 B.c., King Nebuchadnezzar's Babylonian army broke through the defenses of Jerusalem and stopped the sacrifices in the Temple on the 9th of Av. The Jewish calendar is lunar and the month of Av would correspond with the months of July and August. Over six hundred years later, the Roman army under General

Titus broke through the defenses of Jerusalem, destroyed the Temple, and ended the sacrifices on the same day, the 9th of Av. Both destructions marked the beginning of the Jewish captivity into the nations. They occurred on the same day! To this day, the 9th of Av is a day of mourning to the Jewish people.

With the nation of Israel reborn, the times of the Gentile's rule over Jerusalem is drawing to a close. The events now transpiring are all leading to the final climax between the God of Israel and the nations of the world which have rejected His Word. The final world battle recorded in the Bible will take place over Jerusalem and the land of Israel. All the nations of the world will be involved in this final conflict.

Chapter 3
This Land That Was Desolate

And they shall say, This land that was desolate is become
like the garden of Eden; and the waste and desolate and
ruined cities are become fenced, and are inhabited.

—Ezekiel 36:35

The prophet Ezekiel said the Jews would go into all the
nations and the land would be desolate. The worldwide dispersion began in the year 70 when the Temple was
destroyed. There was not a clear indication at the time of
how long the destruction would last. In 136, the Roman
army crushed the second revolt. This time Jerusalem was
totally destroyed, over five hundred thousand Jews were
killed, and the rest were sold into slavery throughout the
Roman Empire. The Romans even changed the name of
the area to Philestina. This is where the modern name Palestine originated. The covenant of God was fulfilled. The
nation was destroyed and the Jews had been scattered into
all the world.

The destruction of the nation continued century after
century with no end in sight. Empire after empire ruled
the area. There was always a small remnant of Jews living
on the land and especially in Jerusalem. From 70 onward,
although the nation was destroyed, a remnant of Jews always lived on the land. Jerusalem was never the capital of
another nation. The nations that ruled over Jerusalem from
the year 70 follows:

1. Romans and Byzantines ruled until 638. Romans first called the land Palestine.
2. Muslims capture Israel and Jerusalem in 638. This began the rule over the area by the Muslim caliphs and the religion of Islam. They ruled until 1072.
3. Seljukes ruled from 1072 until 1096.
4. Crusaders ruled from 1096 until 1291.
5. Mamelukes ruled from 1291 until 1516.
6. Ottoman Turks ruled from 1516 until 1918. This ended the rule of Islam over the area of Israel.
7. British given mandate to rule after WWI from 1918 until May 14, 1948.
8. From May 14 to the present, the nation was once again under Jewish control. In June 1967, all of Jerusalem came under the authority of the nation of Israel. In July 1980, Jerusalem officially became the capital of Israel. Jerusalem was again the capital, as it was nearly three thousand years ago under King David.

The land was invaded by the Romans, Byzantines, Persians, Arabs, Kurds, Mamelukes, Mongols, Tartars, Crusaders, Turks, French, and British. Through all of these wars and conquests, there was a continual Jewish presence on the land. There never was another sovereign nation on the land of Israel or a country that had its capital as Jerusalem. Even under the rule of the Ottoman Turks, Jerusalem was a desolate city with Damascus as the provincial capital over it. God seems to have preserved the land as a nation for His covenant people and Jerusalem as the capital. All of those empires came and went, but the Jews reestablished their homeland. Nothing in history seemed to have prevented the rebirth of the nation.

The modern rebirth of the nation can be traced to the

1880s. Pogroms in Russia against the Jews started a trickle migration seeking peace in Israel. In the 1890s, a trial in France triggered the modern Zionist movement. This incident sparked the return of the Jews in great numbers back to Israel and the rebirth of the nation.

In 1894, Captain Alfred Dreyfus, an intelligence officer on the French general staff, was convicted of spying for Germany. Dreyfus was the only Jew on the general staff, and it became apparent that he was framed. The trial brought a tremendous wave of anti-Semitism from the French people. The trial was followed all over the world. Theodor Herzl, a Jewish journalist from Switzerland, covered this trial. He observed the irrational hatred of the Jews in France this trial caused because Dreyfus was Jewish. In 1896, Herzl published his book *The Jewish State: A Modern Solution to the Jewish Question*. This book called for the creation of a Jewish state, and it led to the founding of the Zionist Organization. The first Zionist Congress met in 1897. This meeting set the economic foundation for the modern state of Israel. Hatred for Jews in France and Russia set the stage for the rebirth of Israel.

The Jews trickled back to Israel through the early part of the twentieth century. The land was owned by the Turks, and Jews bought whatever land they could. In 1914, WWI started. By November 1917 it was apparent that the Turks were going to be defeated by the British in the Middle East. The Ottoman Empire was coming to an end. In anticipating this defeat and the Turks losing control over the covenant land, British foreign secretary Arthur James Balfour issued what is now the famous Balfour Declaration. This rather short document recognized the right of the Jewish people to return to Israel as a homeland. It seems that WWI prepared the land for the return of the Jewish people. The Balfour Declaration follows:

November 2nd, 1917

Dear Lord Rothschild,

I have much pleasure in conveying to you, on behalf
of His Majesty's Government, the following declaration
of sympathy with Jewish Zionist aspirations which has
been submitted to, and approved by, the Cabinet.

"His Majesty's Government view with favour the
establishment in Palestine of a national home for the
Jewish people, and will use their best endeavors to facilitate the achievement of this object, it being clearly
understood that nothing shall be done which may preju-
dice the civil and religious rights of existing non-Jewish
communities in Palestine, or the rights and political status enjoyed by Jews in any other country."

I should be grateful if you would bring this declaration to the knowledge of the Zionist Federation.

Yours sincerely,

Arthur James Balfour

On December 9, 1917, British general Edmund Allenby
captured Jerusalem. General Allenby understood the significance of capturing Jerusalem. He gave orders that
Jerusalem was not to be taken by force. His army was not
to shell or fight in Jerusalem. The Turks retreated from
Jerusalem without firing a shot. Jerusalem and the covenant land fell to the British. For the first time in over six
hundred years the land was no longer under the control of
Islamic nations. After the war, the League of Nations placed
Britain in charge of Israel.

The Muslims refused to recognize the right of the Jews
to a homeland and they rioted. The Arabs put pressure on
the British government to restrict Jewish emigration. There
were Arab riots throughout the 1920s and 1930s. In 1929

for example, all the Jews were massacred in the city of Hebron. The riots pressured the British to reduce the original land grant they had planned for the nation of Israel. The rebirth of the nation was not going to be easy. The Muslim resistance that started in the 1920s has continued to this day. There has been continual fighting over the covenant land to our very day.

The covenant with Abraham, Isaac, and Jacob over the land was not recognized by the Muslims. The establishment of the nation of Israel was going to be difficult, but God's Word clearly stated it was going to happen. No force on earth could stop the rebirth of Israel. God has to fulfill the promise and bring about His redemption of mankind. Israel and Jerusalem both play a key role in this plan. The foundation for the nation was laid in 1917.

World War II was the next big step in the rebirth of Israel. Following the horrors of the Nazis and the defeat of Germany, the United Nations was created. In 1947, the UN voted to partition Palestine into two sections. Jordan was for the Arabs and Israel was for the Jews. The creation of the nation of Israel took effect on May 14, 1948. The Nazi Holocaust of the Jews drove many of the surviving Jews out of Europe. They wanted to go to Israel. By 1948, there were approximately six hundred thousand Jews in Israel. It seems that WWII prepared the Jewish people for the land.

The two world wars of the twentieth century had an enormous impact on the rebirth of Israel. World War I broke the hold of Islam over the area and prepared the land for the rebirth. World War II prepared the heart of the people to want to go back to the land. Remember, God works in the affairs of the nations to fulfill His covenant with Abraham, Isaac, and Jacob. The horrors of the Nazis could not stop the rebirth of Israel. In fact, the atrocities seemed to accelerate the establishment of the nation.

These wars were used to aid directly in the creation of Israel. Hitler tried to destroy world Jewry. Yet, just three years after the defeat of the Nazis, Israel was reborn! The Nazi empire was in ashes, while Israel became a nation. What the Nazis did to the Jews was a direct cause for the creation of Israel. God told Ezekiel that He would cause the Jewish people to leave the nations and come back to Israel. The horrors of World War II was one of the main forces that drove the Jews back to Israel. The Jews were driven from the land by the sword, and in many respects it was the sword that drove them back home.

On May 14, 1948, five Arab nations attacked in an attempt to destroy the newly formed nation of Israel. Israel took no aggressive action against the Arabs, but the mere existence of the Jewish state was enough for the Arabs to attack. The Arab nations of Egypt, Syria, Iraq, Jordan, and Saudi Arabia all attacked. These combined armies were defeated and the nation survived its very difficult rebirth. When the war ended, Israel was an area about eight thousand square miles, or the size of New Jersey. The war ended with the Jews in control of about two-thirds of Jerusalem. Jordan controlled the rest of the city, including the Temple Mount. The majority of the land for the nation of Israel came from two sources. The Jews bought the land. When Turkey was defeated, it turned over to the British tracts of state-owned land. Britain then turned this land over to the newly formed state of Israel.

In 1967, war again broke out. This war became known as the Six-Day War. In May 1967, Egypt and Syria mobilized their armies and threatened to attack Israel. The Egyptian army crossed the Suez Canal and headed toward Israel. Egypt demanded that the United Nations peacekeepers in the Sinai leave, and Egypt closed the Gulf of Aqaba to Israeli shipping. This action by Egypt was an act of war.

On June 5, the Israeli army attacked Egypt and Syria. The Egyptian and Syrian armies were crushed. On the last day of the war, Jordan attacked Israel. In one day, Jordan lost Jerusalem and all the land west of the Jordan River. The tiny nation of Israel had become a world military power in only twenty years of existence.

As the ancient prophets stated, Israel was reborn and Jerusalem was the capital. For the first time since 606 B.C., Jerusalem was once again the capital of an independent Israel. Jesus Christ said that Jerusalem was God's prophetic time piece. Just as Jesus had said, all of Jerusalem was again under complete Jewish control. God's unseen hand was working in the affairs of men to fulfill the everlasting covenant.

The fighting over the land continued. In 1973, Syria and Egypt once again attacked Israel in what is now known as the Yom Kippur War. The attack was a complete surprise. Israel was attacked on one of its holiest days. The nation was nearly defeated, but survived the initial surprise attack. When a truce was declared, the Israeli army was advancing on both Cairo and Damascus.

The land continued to be a source of turmoil. There has been continued fighting over the land. The attacks on Israel from Lebanon caused war in the 1980s. There was rioting and terrorist attacks by the Palestinians in the 1980s and 1990s. On September 28, 2000, fighting broke out in Jerusalem over the Temple Mount. This fighting expanded to a low grade war between Israel and the Palestinians. This fighting has the possibility to escalate into a regional war using weapons of mass destruction that could destroy entire nations. The covenant land of Israel has become the source of world attention just as the Bible said it would. God's prophetic Word is right on target.

Chapter 4

The Latter Day Is Today

Afterward shall the children of Israel return, and seek the LORD their God, and David their king; and shall fear the LORD and his goodness in the latter days.

—Hosea 3:5

The prophet Hosea said in the latter day the Jews would return. Ezekiel also said they would return to Israel in the latter years. Ezekiel describes the latter day as the time when the Jews returned to Israel and the nation was reborn. It would be the time when the Jews came back from the nations of the world and to the covenant land which had been continually a waste land. For centuries upon centuries, the land had been waste and the Jews scattered throughout the world.

Ezekiel puts the latter day in the context of the Jews returning after a worldwide dispersion. Ezekiel describes a huge army that is going to attack Israel. He then identifies the time when this tremendous confederation of nations is going to attack. It will be in the latter years when the Jews are back after the dispersion into the nations.

After many days thou [invading army] shalt be visited [mustered]: in the **latter years** thou shalt come into the land that is brought back from the sword, and is gathered out of many people, against the mountains of Israel, which have been always waste: but it is brought forth out of the nations, and they shall dwell safely all of them.

—Ezekiel 38:8

The Jews are back and the nation of Israel has become a reality. The land for centuries was a true wasteland. It had been defoliated of trees and was full of malarial swamps. The area was poor, with little agriculture. When the Jews left, a curse seemed to have settled on the land. Now, with the Jews back on the land, it is again flourishing. Millions of trees have been planted. The swamps were drained. Israel has wonderful agriculture and supplies Europe with much of its fruit. In fifty years, Israel has become a world military power with nuclear weapons. The rebirth of Israel is no fluke of history. Israel is fulfilling the covenant God made with Abraham four thousand years ago.

Israel can be viewed as just another nation, but this is a mistake. If one was to have predicted any time prior to one hundred years ago that the Jews would return to Israel from all over the world; Jerusalem would again be the capital; the land would produce incredible agriculture; and the nation would be a world military power, few if any would believe. Such a prophecy would have seemed incredible. This is exactly what has happened! If you look at the Bible and history, the modern nation of Israel is supernatural.

There is no nation in history that was twice destroyed. The capital and religious center was twice destroyed. The people en masse were twice taken captive off the land. The last captivity was for nineteen hundred years. The language was all but extinct. For this nation then to be reborn and have the same capital has to be seen as supernatural! The people even speak the same language and have the same religion.

What force has kept this people as a nation even though they were scattered into all the world for nineteen hundred years? What force kept the language and religion intact? What force has kept the Jew from being completely destroyed through pogroms, crusades, holocausts, and all the other attempts to destroy them? The Jew and the nation of Israel are an enigma unless you understand the Bible. The rebirth of the nation shows the authority of the Bible as the Word of God. It shows the invisible hand of God working to fulfill His Word. The everlasting covenant is in effect. God's covenant is that force which has kept Israel through the centuries. According to the Bible, this is the latter days. "And I will plant them upon their land, and they shall no more be pulled up out of their land which I have given them, saith the LORD thy God" (Amos 9:15).

Chapter 5

Israel: God's Anvil

The words of the LORD are pure words: as silver tried in
a furnace of earth, purified seven times.

—Psalm 12:6

The rebirth of the nation of Israel has been a real slow
process. The process started in the late 1800s and has
continued right up to the present time. At times, this process seems to stop, and then all of sudden a huge event
takes place that accelerates it. The start of the Jews coming
back did not seem significant at first. But, there was a small
but steady stream of them. Then came WWI, and in 1917
the Balfour Declaration. Then like an explosion, the land
was being readied for the return.

The period between world wars was one of tension and
terrorism. There was no apparent move of God toward fulfilling the covenant. Then came WWII and the Nazi Holocaust. The events of WWII set the stage for hundreds of
thousands of Jews to go back to Israel. Almost like an explosion, there were huge numbers of Jews ready to go back
to Israel.

Then came the rebirth of the nation in 1948 and the
immediate war. The war ended and Israel was once again
faced with tension and terrorism. For twenty years, there
seemed no end to the shelling and terrorists attacks. Then
came the Six-Day War in 1967, and like a bolt of lightning,

Israel had all of a united Jerusalem as its capital. Since 1967, there has been a major war, plus fighting in Lebanon and continual terrorist attacks against Israel. Starting in September 2000, a low-grade war was started over Jerusalem. This war is a continuation of the fighting that started in 1920. Although the fighting and terrorism seem endless, there will be an end. Between the major moves to restore Israel, it seems tension, terrorism, and fighting were always prevalent.

It has been almost forty years since Jerusalem was united. Now, the fighting is directly over Jerusalem and the Temple Mount area. The Bible states that the last great world war will be over Jerusalem. All the nations of the world will be drawn to Jerusalem. God is going to use Jerusalem as an anvil against the nations of the world. The fuse to start the last world war may have been lit in September 2000 when the Temple Mount became the scene of bloody combat.

God is moving to fulfill the promises of His everlasting covenant, but one has to be patient. God seems to have moved very slowly with Israel to completely fulfill the promise. Looking back, since 1917 tremendous progress has been made. Israel is a nation with Jerusalem as the capital. Israel is a mighty military power. Israel has a powerful economy. The rest of the promises of the covenant will be fulfilled in God's time.

No matter what was tried by the British, Muslims, United Nations, European Union, or any other group, their attempts have not been able to stop the rebirth of the nation. Israel is truly like an anvil, and nations are going to be broken trying to destroy God's covenant nation. In watching God working, great patience is required. The restoration has taken almost a century to get this far. God has His own agenda and timetable. Watching Jerusalem and the war that started in September 2000 over the Temple Mount shows that God's timetable may be accelerating. Remember, Jesus Christ said that Jerusalem was the key to the timetable.

With the rebirth of Israel and Jerusalem the capital, this nation becomes an anvil for false views of God and Bible doctrine. Most religions of the world do not recognize God's covenant over the land of Israel. Some believe the Jews had a covenant, but this covenant is no longer in effect. God is using Israel to now show the literalness of His Word. The rebirth of Israel confronts false teaching, doctrine, and prophets. Israel has become an anvil to break the false doctrines and misunderstandings of the Bible.

Islam does not recognize the covenant with Isaac and Jacob, but instead believes God made a covenant with Abraham and Ishmael. Islam believes the Koran and not the Bible is the word of God. The Koran fails to mention Jerusalem even once, and it does not mention the rebirth of the nation of Israel. Jerusalem is mentioned eight hundred and eleven times in the Bible. The rebirth of Israel is on page after page in the Bible, while the Koran is silent. The rebirth of Israel shows the authority of the Bible as the Word of God. God's everlasting covenant and the rebirth of Israel is like an anvil against the Koran. Israel is proof the Koran and Mohammed are wrong.

This tension between Israel and the Koran can never be peacefully resolved. For Islam to recognize the nation of Israel would be an admission that the Koran and Islam are wrong. Muslim fundamentalists refer to Israel as the "Zionist entity." They will not even recognize the nation of Israel. There is a huge confrontation on the horizon between the God of the Bible and Islam. The heart of the confrontation will be the Jewish control of Jerusalem. God is using Israel as an anvil against Islam. When the Islamic nations

come against Israel and Jerusalem, they will be destroyed.
God is using Israel as an anvil against false teachings
within the Christian church. There are doctrines called replacement theology and covenant theology. Both these doctrines are fluid and there are many branches to them; however, believers hold the church has now replaced Israel in
the everlasting covenant. These doctrines hold that God has
no future plan with the nation of Israel, and when Israel
was destroyed in A.D. 70, it ended the everlasting covenant.
Israel then fell under the curse of the law, but all the blessings in the Bible now belong to the church. These doctrines
are in stark contrast to what the prophet Jeremiah states.
Jeremiah claims that the nation of Israel will remain forever:

> Thus saith the LORD, which giveth the sun for a light by
> day, and the ordinances of the moon and of the stars for
> a light by night, which divideth the sea when the waves
> thereof roar; The LORD of hosts is his name: If those ordi-
> nances depart from before me, saith the LORD, then the
> seed of Israel also shall cease from being a nation before
> me for ever. Thus saith the LORD; If heaven above can be
> measured, and the foundations of the earth searched out
> beneath, I will also cast off all the seed of Israel for all
> that they have done, saith the LORD.
>
> —Jeremiah 31:35–37

God has used the rebirth of Israel to prove both these doctrines to be incorrect. Just as Moses and the prophets have
said, the physical descendants have returned and the nation was reborn. The Bible is to be taken literally about
Jerusalem meaning Jerusalem, Israel meaning Israel, and
not spiritualizing it to say Jerusalem and Israel now mean
the church.

To try and get around the error of the replacement and covenant theology, some believers in these doctrines have gone so far as to say the Jews in Israel are not real Jews. When these "Jews" were being killed in pogroms in Russia, no one said, "Stop, they are not real Jews." When these "Jews" were being killed by the Nazis, no one said, "Stop, they are not real Jews." Now, when these same "Jews" go back to Israel, all of a sudden they are no longer Jews.

God is using the rebirth of Israel to cut right through false and incorrect views of His Word. The promise of God in the Bible is crystal clear on page after page. Man-made doctrines and false prophets have tried to alter this covenant, but in the latter day, God has made the truth clear for all to see. God is very serious about His Word. "Then said the LORD unto me, Thou hast well seen: for I will hasten my word to perform it" (Jeremiah 1:12).

Believing in false doctrines about the literalness of the rebirth of Israel blinds people to the working of God that is occurring right before their eyes. God is moving to fulfill His Word, and millions cannot see it because they are following false prophets or wrong doctrines about Israel and Jerusalem. The very sad part is believers in Jesus Christ, because of false doctrine, can actually be against the work of God. Many fail to support God's covenant nation and can be against it because of a false understanding of Israel and the everlasting covenant.

It is very serious to be on the wrong side of God when He is defending His everlasting covenant. The wrong doctrine can cause a person to be apathetic toward Israel and the Jews. This can lead to the failure to pray for and support Israel in a time of crisis. This incorrect doctrine blinds a person's ability to see God's judgment falling on America for forcing Israel.

God is real serious about the land and covenant. Israel

will literally be used as an anvil to destroy the nations that come against Jerusalem. The nations will be drawn to Jerusalem like a moth to a light. Multitudes of people have rejected God and the Bible or just do not believe His Word. This rebellion will cause the nations to come against God's anvil. God has warned beforehand what will happen when armies try to destroy Israel and take Jerusalem. The entire world will see the mighty power of God, as He uses Israel as His anvil. This is all laid out in the Bible, and will be covered in depth in the chapter titled "Jerusalem a Burdensome Stone for the Nations."

God is using the rebirth of Israel like an anvil to expose false prophets, doctrines, and to have a literal witness on the earth to the authority of His Word. It is important that one's faith be in accord with the truth of the Bible.

God's Word has been tested in the furnace of the earth. The Word has proven itself to be like pure gold and silver. The everlasting covenant has been tested now for four thousand years of history. It is, in effect, for all to see. God is faithful to His Word and promises. His Word is pure for all to see. "The words of the LORD are pure words: as silver tried in a furnace of earth, purified seven times" (Psalm 12:6).

Chapter 6

America: Blessed or Cursed?

And I will bless them that bless thee, and curse him that
curseth thee. . . .

—Genesis 12:3

Nearly every day, Israel is in the news. Israel and especially Jerusalem has become the focus of world attention. Israel has been the subject of a large percentage of the United Nations resolutions. These resolutions were from both the General Assembly and the Security Council. In 1997, the United Nations voted five times to condemn Israel for merely building apartments in East Jerusalem. Nearly all the countries of the world voted against Israel.

The land of Israel and especially Jerusalem are literally the focus of world attention. The peace plan in the Middle East involves Israel giving disputed land to the Palestinians for peace. This plan was initiated in 1991 by President George H. W. Bush and continued until September 2000. The disputed land is called the West Bank, Gaza, and the Golan Heights. This peace plan also involves Israel giving East Jerusalem to the Palestinians as their capital. The ruins of the ancient Jewish Temple are located in East Jerusalem.

The world is so sensitive about Jerusalem that in 1980 when Israel moved its capital from Tel Aviv to Jerusalem, most nations refused to recognize Jerusalem as the capital of Israel. The nations kept their embassies in Tel Aviv!

Through the United Nations and the American initiated peace plan, there is tremendous pressure on Israel over the land.

Even though the nations of the world are politically against Israel, this country is totally unique. Israel is the only country in the world in which the land was a promise by God. The nation of Israel is based on the faithfulness of God's promise in the Bible.

The prophet Joel said that God will judge the nations that have touched the Jewish people and parted the land of the nation of Israel.

> For, behold, in those days, and in that time, when I shall bring again the captivity of Judah and Jerusalem, I will also gather all nations, and will bring them down into the valley of Jehoshaphat, and will plead [punish, judge] with them there for my people and for my heritage Israel, whom they have scattered among the nations, and parted [divided] my land.
>
> —Joel 3: 1–2.

The prophet Zechariah said that God will defend Israel and Jerusalem. God will destroy the nations that come against Jerusalem, even though all the nations of the earth be gathered against it. Jerusalem will be the center of world attention and military action:

> Behold, I will make Jerusalem a cup of trembling unto all the people round about, when they shall be in the siege both against Judah and against Jerusalem. And in that day will I make Jerusalem a burdensome stone for all people: all that burden themselves with it shall be cut in pieces, though all the people of the earth be gathered together against it.
>
> —Zechariah 12:2–3

And it shall come to pass in that day, that I will seek to
destroy all the nations that come against Jerusalem.

                                    —Zechariah 12:9.

In 1991, George W. H. Bush led America to victory over
Iraq in the Desert Storm War. Following the war, President
Bush took it upon himself to have a comprehensive peace
plan for the Middle East. In October 1991 he convened the
Madrid peace process. The heart of this peace plan involved
Israel and the covenant land. President George Bush using
the might of the United States literally forced Israel into
this peace process with the Palestinians and Syrians. The
heart of the peace process was for Israel to give land for
peace. The term "peace plan" was a code that meant Israel
must give up land. The land to be given away was part of
the land grant God had given Abraham, Isaac, and Jacob.

In 1993 the Madrid peace plan evolved into the Oslo
accords. The Oslo accords set a timetable for Israel's with-
drawal from parts of the covenant land. The Oslo accords
also focused on the issue of Jerusalem. By 1998, seven
years after the peace process started, the center of the land
to be given away became Jerusalem. The United States became the prime force in this peace process of pressuring
Israel to give away its land. The Bible says God will judge
the nations which have parted the land of Israel. The city
of Jerusalem will become a burdensome stone, and the
nations will be cut in pieces as they come against it.

The United States has come against Jerusalem and has
challenged God's Word. In November 1991 President Bush
Sr. started the peace process and President Clinton continued it, and now President George W. Bush has been left
with following through. President Clinton had pressured
Israel to give away large sections of the land, and he made
Jerusalem negotiable. He had condemned Israel for build-

ing apartments in East Jerusalem. Presidents Bush Sr. and Clinton have brought America into a confrontation with God over the land of Israel and Jerusalem. President George W. Bush has endorsed the Mitchell Plan for Israel. The Mitchell Plan calls for Israel to stop all building activity in the settlements in the West Bank and get back to the peace talks. Of course, these peace talks mean Israel will be required to give up parts of the covenant land.

Since November 1991, God has warned America that the nation was on a collision course with Him over Jerusalem. As America has pressured Israel to give away land, warning-judgments have hit. These warning-judgments have occurred through all three presidencies. They resulted in some of the greatest disasters in the nation's history. The disasters have fallen on the very day of forcing Israel over the land or Jerusalem.

God warns that whosoever touches Israel touches the apple (pupil) of His eye. The pupil is one of the most delicate and sensitive parts of the body. A person will immediately move to defend the pupil from an object that comes near to it. This is the picture that God gives to His reaction of touching His covenant nation. There will be a reaction from God. The following are examples of the warning–judgments which have occurred as the United States has pressured Israel to give away land and interfered with Jerusalem. America has touched the "apple of God's eye."

The Results of Touching the Apple of God's Eye
November 1991
After the Gulf War ended in 1991, President Bush began the initiative to start a Middle East peace plan involving Israel, the Palestinians, and the countries surrounding Israel. The talks were scheduled to begin on October 30, 1991, in Madrid, Spain. On October 30, 1991, President Bush

opened the talks with a speech. In this speech the president said that "territorial compromise is essential for peace." From the very start of the Madrid peace process, the president was very clear that Israel would have to give away part of the covenant land for peace. The very foundation of this peace process was Israel giving away the covenant land. An excerpt of the president's speech follows:

> Throughout the Middle East, we seek a stable and enduring settlement. We've not defined what this means. Indeed, I make these points with no map showing where the final borders are to be drawn. Nevertheless we believe territorial compromise is essential for peace.

On October 30, in their opening speeches the Egyptian, Syrian, and Palestinian delegations said that for peace Israel must give away land. At the very beginning of these talks, the land of Israel was the key issue. The Egyptian foreign minister, Amr Moussa, summarized the Arab position regarding the land of Israel and peace. He listed four points that had to be addressed, three of which dealt with the land of Israel. An excerpt of Mr. Moussa's speech follows:

> Secondly, the West Bank, Gaza and the Golan Heights are occupied territories.
>
> Thirdly, settlements established in territories occupied since '67, including Jerusalem are illegal, and more settlements will foreclose potential progress toward real peace and cast doubts on the credibility of the process itself.
>
> Fourthly, the holy city of Jerusalem has its special status. . . . The occupying power should not exercise monopoly or illegal sovereignty over the holy city. It should not persist in unilateral decisions declared to annex the

holy city as this lacks validity or legitimacy.

On October 30, a powerful storm developed off Nova Scotia. The storm was never classified as a hurricane because its sustained winds reached only 73 mph. To be classified as a hurricane, the sustained winds have to be 74 mph. This storm was extremely rare, because it traveled for one thousand miles in a eastward to westward direction. The weather pattern for the United States is westward to eastward. The storm was called extratropical because it did not originate in the tropics, as most hurricanes do.

On October 31, this ferocious storm smashed into New England. The storm was described as a monster, as it was hundreds of miles wide. This storm was later called "the Perfect Storm," and a book was written and a movie was made about this storm. The book and movie were both called *The Perfect Storm*. The Perfect Storm was described by meteorologists as one of the most powerful storms to have ever occurred!

Extremely rare weather patterns that happen once every one hundred years came together to create this monster storm. The ocean waves were over one hundred feet high, which were the highest ever recorded. The Perfect Storm ran down the East Coast into the Carolinas, doing hundreds of millions of dollars in damage. The storm damaged the entire East Coast from Maine to Florida. Remember, this storm was going the wrong way! The damage caused by the Perfect Storm was classified with that of powerful hurricanes.

The Perfect Storm even heavily damaged President Bush's home in Kennebunkport, Maine. Eyewitnesses said that waves as high as thirty feet smashed into the president's seafront home. The president had to cancel speaking engagements to go and inspect the damage done to his home.

As President Bush was speaking in Madrid, an extremely rare and powerful storm developed in the North Atlantic Ocean. The storm then struck the entire East Coast from Maine to Florida as the Madrid peace conference was taking place. The storm even heavily damaged the president's personal home!

The front page headlines of the *New York Times* and *USA Today* newspapers on November 1 even had the Madrid conference and the Perfect Storm next to each other! The *USA Today*'s articles were titled "One-on-one peace talks next." The article touching was titled "East Coast hit hard by rare storm."

At the very beginning of the peace plan involving Israel, a rare and powerful storm smashes into the entire East Coast of the United States. The Perfect Storm heavily damaged President Bush's home, who was the initiator of the Madrid peace plan. The connection between dividing the land of Israel and judgment on the nation causing it was tied together on the front page of America's largest national newspaper. On October 31, 1991, America was put on notice by the Lord God of Israel.

August 1992

On August 23, 1992, the Madrid peace conference moved to Washington, D.C., and the talks resumed. The nations involved felt the United States was a better location to continue the talks. The key issue remained that Israel had to give away land for peace. The U.S. representative was acting Secretary of State Lawrence Eagleburger. The *New York Times* reported an interview with Eagleburger about the opening of the Madrid Peace talks in Washington and part of the interview follows:

The peace talks were resuming "in the context of an Israeli Government that is prepared to be far more forth coming." He predicted that the issue of Palestinian self-rule in the Israeli-occupied territories would be the focus of discussion.

On August 23, 1992, Hurricane Andrew smashed into southern Florida. Hurricane Andrew was the worst natural disaster ever to hit America. It left 180,000 in Florida homeless and another 25,000 in Louisiana. The damage was estimated as high as $30 billion. This was an awesome category four hurricane with top winds recorded at 175 mph; however the wind measuring device was destroyed before the eye hit. The winds may have been as high as 200 mph! This storm was described by the National Hurricane Center as a 25- to 30-mile wide tornado!

Hurricane Andrew hit the day the Madrid peace conference met in Washington, D.C. One of the greatest natural disasters ever in American history hit the very day of the conference for Israel to give away its land took place. This conference was originated by President Bush and now moved to American soil.

On August 24, the front-page headlines of the *USA Today* newspaper were "1 Million flee Andrew," "This will make Hugo look weak," and "Monster storm targets Fla." Also, on the front page was an article titled "Mideast peace talks to resume on positive note." America again was hit with a powerful natural disaster in direct connection with the Madrid peace plan.

On August 24, the front page of the *New York Times* also had articles about Hurricane Andrew and the Madrid peace plan meetings. The Madrid meeting article was at the top in the very center of the front page while the hurricane story was directly to the right. Directly to the left of the Madrid peace plan article was a story about President Bush's ratings collapsing in the polls. Bill Clinton was leading in the polls by a substantial margin. Just a year before,

President Bush had a tremendous approval rating.

Following the victory over Iraq in February 1991, President Bush's rating were as high as ninety-two percent. In October 1991 he personally initiated the Madrid peace plan and forced Israel into the negotiations. In less than one year he had crashed in the polls and was heading to reelection defeat. The irony of this is President Bush's crashing in the polls coincided with the Madrid peace process meeting in Washington, D.C. He initiated the peace process in 1991, and when the meeting first took place on American soil in 1992, his popularity was crashing.

Three major events converged on the same day. The Madrid peace process meeting for the first time on American soil; the destruction caused by Hurricane Andrew; and the collapse of the presidency of George W. H. Bush. The man who initiated the plan forcing Israel to give away land was removed from office almost exactly one year after the beginning of the meetings. His political collapse was apparent for all to see at the exact time the peace process moved to America! The timing of all this was breath taking.

The connection between dividing the land of Israel and God's judgment concerning it was right on the front page of the nation's largest national newspapers. God is not hiding anything.

September 1993

On September 1, 1993, the front-page headline of the *New York Times* newspaper was "Israel and PLO Ready to Declare Joint Recognition." The subtitle was "Meet Secretly in Europe." The article went on to say that diplomatic action was going on secretly in Europe. The agreement reached became known as the Oslo peace accords. This agreement was that Israel would give away Gaza and Jericho to the Palestinians, followed quickly by the rest of the

West Bank. In return, the Palestinians would agree to recognize the state of Israel and live in peace. This peace plan was to come to a conclusion within seven years, ending in September 2000.

The agreement was to be signed in Washington on September 13, 1993, by Yasser Arafat and Israeli prime minister Yitzhak Rabin. The issue of Jerusalem was not addressed at this time, but was put off for two years.

Also, on the front page as a headline was an article titled "Hurricane Hits Outer Banks as Thousands Seek Safety Inland." Hurricane Emily had meandered across the Atlantic Ocean for five days, but finally hit North Carolina the very day of the peace accord agreement! This hurricane had 115 mph winds. It brushed the coast of North Carolina, and it then turned and headed out to sea. The damage caused by this hurricane was light.

This was the third hurricane to hit the United States on the very day of a key event of the peace process for Israel to give away land. The headline articles about the hurricane and Israel were actually touching each other! This is another clear warning from God broadcasted on the front page of a national newspaper, that the nation is on a collision course with Him over the land of Israel!

January 1994

On January 16, 1994, President Clinton met with Syria's president Hafez Assad in Geneva. They met to discuss peace between Israel and Syria. President Clinton said Syria was ready for a peace agreement with Israel that would include Israel giving the Golan Heights to Syria. (The Golan is the border between Syria and Israel. In 1967, during the war with Syria, Israel gained this territory. This is part of the land God gave to Abraham.) The newspapers quoted President Clinton as saying, "Israel must make concessions that will be politically unpopular with many Israelis."

Less than twenty-four hours later, a powerful 6.9 earthquake rocked southern California. This earthquake was centered in Northridge about twenty-five miles from Los Angeles. The quake was the second most destructive natural disaster to hit the United States. It was second to Hurricane Andrew.

This earthquake was literally under the feet of the center of the pornography industry of America! It also occurred only a few hours after Sanctity of Life Sunday and a few days before the anniversary of *Roe v. Wade!* The quake also destroyed several abortion centers. (Awesome disasters have hit America on days involving abortion and homosexuality. For a complete study of the disasters related to abortion and homosexuality, see John McTernan's book *God's Final Warning to America.*)

Less than twenty-four hours after President Clinton was pressuring Israel to give away land, America was rocked by a powerful and damaging earthquake. This occurred only hours after Sanctity of Life Sunday! What an awesome warning-judgment to America. This earthquake hit in direct connection to abortion, pornography, and forcing Israel to part the land! Some of the greatest natural disasters to hit America—Hurricane Andrew and the Northridge earthquake—occurred exactly on the days America was pressuring Israel to give away its land.

God warns in the Bible that He will judge nations as they deal with Israel. It is crystal clear that America has come under the judgment hand of God for its dealings with the nation of Israel!

March–April 1997

On March 1, Yasser Arafat left Israel and arrived in Washington, D.C., to meet with President Clinton. They met to

discuss a Jewish housing project being built in East Jerusalem. This is the section of Jerusalem which is claimed by
the Palestinians. The Israeli government had begun to build
sixty-five hundred housing units in East Jerusalem in an
area called Har Homa. Arafat was upset and met with President Clinton to discuss this issue.

Arafat was given a warm welcome by President Clinton.
The *New York Times* reported the meeting with this article:
"Welcoming Arafat, Clinton Rebukes Israel." The president
rebuked Israel for building the housing in Jerusalem, and
he condemned Israel for creating mistrust.

Arafat went on a speaking tour of the United States and
was warmly received. He spoke in the United Nations about
the situation in Jerusalem. In one speech he used the example of the Vatican in Rome as an example of what should
happen in Jerusalem—a Palestinian city within Jerusalem.

The issue of Israel building homes in Jerusalem upset
the entire world. On five separate occasions between March
6 and July 15, the United Nations Security Council and the
General Assembly voted to condemn Israel for building
homes in East Jerusalem. The entire world was upset because Jews were building houses Jerusalem! A percentage
of these homes were to be for Arabs.

On March 6, the Security Council voted to strongly criti-
cize Israel. The resolution said that the housing was a violation of international law and a threat to peace in the Mideast. The United States vetoed the resolution, which prevented it from becoming official. Outside of the U.N., the
Clinton administration condemned Israel for the building
project. The issue was then taken to the General Assembly.

On March 13, the General Assembly voted to condemn
Israel over building homes in East Jerusalem. The vote was
130–2 to condemn Israel. Only Israel and the United States
voted against the resolution. Fifty-one nations failed to vote.

The resolution said that the housing was illegal and a major obstacle to peace. This vote showed the strength of feeling as to how unified the world was against Jerusalem. The Clinton administration continued to condemn Israel outside of the U.N. All this international condemnation of Israel was over building homes in Jerusalem!

On March 21, the Security Council again voted to condemn Israel and once again the United States vetoed the resolution. The U.S. criticized Israel outside the U.N. for the housing project. On April 25 the General Assembly demanded by a 134–3 vote that Israel stop the housing project in Jerusalem. The resolution also called for international action against Israel. The U.S. voted against the resolution.

On July 15, the General Assembly again voted by 131–3 for a resolution to condemn Israel for the housing project. This was the strongest resolution yet, as it called for an economic boycott of products made in Jewish settlements in the disputed areas of Israel including Jerusalem. The U.S. voted against this resolution.

From March 1, when Arafat traveled to America until mid-April, Israel was constantly under criticism by the Clinton administration for the housing project in Jerusalem. The U.S. supported Israel in the United Nations, but outside of the U.N., Israel was constantly criticized by President Clinton.

On the very day Arafat landed in America, powerful tornadoes devastated huge sections of the nation. While Arafat was on a speaking tour, which was against Israel, these storms stalled over Ohio and caused tremendous flooding. The tornadoes destroyed Arkadelphia, Arkansas, while the flooding destroyed Falmouth, Kentucky. The storms did over one billion dollars in damage. Also, heavy snows fell in March and April in the Northern Plains. These snows melted and in April caused the worst flooding in a century in the Dakotas. This was also a billion dollar disaster.

While Arafat toured America, some of the worst tornadoes hit, along with awesome floods. Remember, God will judge the nations that divide Israel. Arafat was using America as a platform to promote the dividing of Israel. He was warmly received by President Clinton! The president's own home state was devastated by the tornadoes!

The connection between President Clinton meeting with Arafat and condemning Israel, and the destructive tornadoes that devastated Arkansas was captured by the *New York Times*. On March 4, 1997, the front-page headlines said, "In Storms Wake Grief and Shock." Directly touching this article was a picture of President Clinton with Arafat and the heading of the picture said, "President Clinton Rebukes Israel." The front page of a national newspaper actually had the destruction of the tornadoes and rebuking of Israel touching each other! The *New York Times* put it together so clearly!

On March 11, the stock market reached an all-time high of 7,085 points. The market had been steadily increasing since October 1996. On March 13, the U.N. General Assembly voted overwhelmingly to condemn Israel, and on this day the stock market plunged 160 points. The market continued to plunge until April 13, when it stabilized and then resumed its upward climb. Between March 13 and April 13, the market lost 694 points.

On April 7, President Clinton met with Israeli prime minister Benjamin Netanyahu to discuss the peace process and the building of homes in Jerusalem. This meeting coincided with the plunge in the market. Prime Minister Netanyahu refused to stop the building of the homes in Jerusalem. After this meeting, the attacks against Israel over the land of Jerusalem subsided. President Clinton stopped the condemnation of Israel. Very soon after this, the stock market stabilized.

From March 13, when the General Assembly first condemned Israel, until after the meeting with Netanyahu, the stock market dropped 694 points. The drop in the market and the crisis over Jerusalem were again front-page stories on a national newspaper. On April 3, the *New York Times* front-page article was titled "The Mideast Muddle." A small article touching it was titled "Stock Downturn Resumes."

March and April 1997 were awesome months for God's dealings with America. The combination of Arafat coming to America and Clinton rebuking Israel over not giving away land coincided with some of the worst tornadoes and floods of the last century. It also coincided with the storms in the Dakotas which resulted in the worst flooding ever. Both of these disasters resulted in damages of over a billion dollars. Entire towns were destroyed like Arkadelphia, Arkansas; Falmouth, Kentucky; and Grand Forks, North Dakota. The Bible states God will judge the nations that divide the land of Israel. In March and April, the land of America suffered terribly as pressure was put on Israel.

As the U.N. condemned Israel over Jerusalem, the stock market began to melt down. The very day of the General Assembly's condemnation of Israel over Jerusalem, the market began a month long slide. The U.S. stock market affects the entire world. As the world through the U.N. came against Israel, the world's largest stock market was shaken. It is interesting to note that both Wall Street, the location of the market, and the U.N. are located in New York City. The land of America and the stock market were judged at the same time over Jerusalem.

July 1997
On July 2, Thailand devalued its currency. The world's lead-

ing economic nations paid no attention to this devaluation. However, this act by Thailand began to destabilize the entire world economy. By devaluing its currency, Thailand could handle its debt better. It made Thailand's exports cheaper; thus the nation was more competitive on the world market.

Soon after Thailand devalued its currency, nearly all the nations of Asia did the same. One by one the nations' currencies fell and then their stock markets began to fall. Thailand, South Korea, Philippines, Indonesia, Hong Kong, Japan, and other nations' stock markets began to collapse. By October, the panic spread to America, and on October 27 the stock market fell 554 points. The stock market recovered and resumed its climb toward 10,000.

The world's economy was shaken by this. There were headlines in the newspapers such as, "Market dive circles globe." The devaluation of Thailand's currency in July turned into a world economic crisis only three months later. This crisis affected the world economy and drastic measures were undertaken to prop up these Asian countries. The failure of Japan would shake the entire world economy.

In March and April 1997, the United Nations voted four times to condemn Israel for building homes in Jerusalem. On July 15, 1997, the U.N. General Assembly again voted by 131–3 to condemn Israel for building homes in Jerusalem. This was the strongest resolution against Israel. The resolution called for identifying all products produced in the disputed areas and then to boycott these products. The U.N. had economically come against Israel. While the U.N. was drafting plans against Israel, Thailand devalued its currency on July 2 which started the shaking of the entire world's economy. A very short time later, the entire world economy was in turmoil.

The entire world through the United Nations came

against Israel in March and April 1997. On July 15, 1997, the world tried to punish Israel economically through a boycott. On July 2, the world economy started to unravel. Jerusalem and the land of Israel had taken center stage in world politics. The United Nations wanted the disputed land in Israel given away and Jerusalem divided. As the nations were planning to economically punish Israel, the world economy was shaken. Many nations in Asia were reduced to poverty. The economic meltdown, which started in Asia, then spread to Russia and later Brazil. None of these nations voted to support Israel in the United Nations. As the nations of the world are coming against Israel, they are being destroyed.

"And in that day will I make Jerusalem a burdensome stone for all people: all that burden themselves with it shall be cut in pieces, though all the people of the earth be gathered together against it" (Zechariah 12:3). Jerusalem has become a burdensome stone for the nations, and they are being cut in pieces as they come against *the apple of God's eye.*

January 1998

On January 21, Israeli prime minister Benjamin Netanyahu met with President Clinton. The meeting was to discuss the stalled peace plan and for Israel to give away some of its land. In the lead-up to the meeting, Netanyahu was under tremendous political pressure. Clinton was pressuring Israel to give away the land for the peace process. In Israel, there was pressure on Netanyahu not to give away land. The pressure was so great that politicians in Israel threatened to pull down his government if he gave away the land.

Netanyahu met with Clinton and was coldly received. Clinton and Secretary of State Albright refused to have lunch with him. Shortly after the meeting ended, a sex scandal involving Clinton became headline news. Clinton became totally involved in the scandal and couldn't devote any time to Israel. He met with Arafat the next day, but there was no effort to pressure Israel to give away land.

Netanyahu came to the meeting with the possibility that his government might fall. How ironic that literally right after the meeting, it was President Clinton's administration that was in trouble. The president was humiliated and faced legal action. The very day Clinton was pressuring Israel to give away land was the day he was humiliated in a sex scandal. Netanyahu returned to Israel as a "conquering hero" because he did not give away any land.

Because of this scandal, the legal action against the president continued until he appeared before a grand jury on August 17. After his grand jury appearance, the president addressed the nation and admitted he had misled the grand jury when he testified under oath in January. On September 9, the report of the investigation of the president was sent to the House of Representatives for possible impeachment and removal from office. On October 8, 1998, the House of Representatives voted for an impeachment inquiry of President Clinton. On December 19, 1998, the House of Representatives passed two Articles of Impeachment against President Clinton, and sent the articles to the Senate for a trial.

The sex scandal involving Clinton broke almost five years to the day that he issued five executive orders reversing years of abortion limitations. On the day after his inauguration in 1993 and on the eve of *Roe v. Wade*, he issued these orders. Exactly five years later, almost to the very day, this sex scandal involving the president was international headline news. The sex scandal that rocked the presidency coincided with the anniversary of his abortion executive orders and forcing Israel to give away land!

September 1998

On September 24, 1998, President Clinton announced he was going to meet with Yasser Arafat and Israel's prime minister Benjamin Netanyahu when they both came to New York City to address the United Nations. The purpose of the meeting was to discuss the stalled peace plan in which Israel was to give away an additional thirteen percent of its land. On this same day, the headlines of the national newspapers said that Hurricane Georges was gaining strength and heading toward the Gulf of Mexico. The headlines of *USA Today* stated, "Georges gaining strength, Killer storm zeros in on Key West."

On September 27, Secretary of State Madeleine Albright met with Arafat in New York City in preparation for the meeting with the President. Albright was working out final arrangements for Israel to give away thirteen percent of its land. On September 27, Hurricane Georges slammed into the Gulf Coast with 110 mph winds, with gusts up to 175 mph. The eye of the storm struck Mississippi and did extensive damage eastward into the Florida panhandle. This hurricane hit the coast and then stalled. The hurricane moved very slowly inland and dumped tremendous amounts of rain causing tremendous flooding.

On September 28, President Clinton met with both Arafat and Netanyahu in the White House. The meeting was to finalize Israel giving the land away. The three agreed to meet on October 15 to formally announce the agreement. The headlines of *USA Today* stated, "Georges lingers." The article next to it was, "Meeting puts Mideast talks back in motion." The newspapers actually had the hurricane and Israeli peace talks next to each other on the front page! The *New York Times* also had the hurricane and peace talks together on the front page.

On September 28, Arafat addressed the United Nations

and talked about an independent Palestinian state by May 1999. Arafat was given a rousing and sustained ovation as he addressed the General Assembly. As Arafat was speaking, Hurricane Georges was smashing the Gulf Coast, causing $1 billion in damage! Arafat finished and then left America. Hurricane Georges then dissipated.

The exact time Arafat was in the United States for the purpose of dividing Israel, Hurricane Georges was pounding the Gulf Coast. Arafat left America and the hurricane then dissipated! God judges the nations that divide His land.

October 1998

On October 15, 1998, Yasser Arafat and Benjamin Netanyahu met at Wye Plantation, Maryland, to continue the talks which ended on September 28. The talks where scheduled to last five days and were centered around Israel giving away thirteen percent of the West Bank land. The talks stalled and President Clinton pressured them to continue until a settlement was reached. The talks were extended and concluded on October 23. In the end, Israel agreed to give away the land for assurances of peace by Arafat.

On October 17, awesome rains and tornadoes hit eastern Texas. The San Antonio area was deluged by twenty inches of rain in one day! The rains caused flash floods and destroyed thousands of homes. Rivers swelled to incredible size. The Guadalupe River, which was normally one hundred fifty feet wide, swelled to three to five miles wide. The floods were so powerful that entire small towns were nearly swallowed. The rains and floods continued until October 22 (the end of the Middle East talks) and then subsided. The rains and floods ravaged twenty-five percent of Texas and did over $1 billion in damage.

On October 21, President Clinton declared this section of Texas a major disaster area, and directed Federal Emergency Management Agency (FEMA) to assist in the relief for the flood-ravaged families. This was a record flood that hit Texas.

For almost the entire duration of the Middle East talks, awesome rains and storms were smashing Texas. The national newspapers once again had the Middle East talks and disaster together on the front page! As the talks ended, the storms and flooding in Texas ended. Once again President Clinton had to declare a section of America a disaster area—at the exact time he was meeting with Arafat to divide Israel!

November 1998

The stock market recovered from the crash of July–September and went on to record levels. The week of November 23 the market reached its all time high. On November 30, Arafat came to Washington, D.C., and met with President Clinton. Arafat came to raise money for his Palestinian state, and he also said that in May 1999 he was going to declare a Palestinian state with Jerusalem as the capital.

A total of forty-two other nations were represented at this meeting in Washington. All the nations together agreed to give Arafat $3 billion in aid. President Clinton promised that the United States would give $400 million and the European nations pledged $1.7 billion.

As President Clinton was meeting with Arafat, the stock market was crashing, and it fell for a total of 216 points this day. The economic pundits could not explain why the stock market crashed other than for profit taking. The radio news reports for November 30 had the Mideast meeting and the stock market crash as stories following each other. The meeting and the crash were headline stories the next day in some of the nation's newspapers. The articles were even touching each other on the front page.

On December 1, the European stock markets crashed for the third worst crash in European history. How ironic that as the nations of the world met to promise $3 billion dollars in aid for a Palestinian state, their own stock markets crashed! This happened literally to the day for the United States and the very next day for Europe.

As the nations of the world continue to come against God's covenant land of Israel and Jerusalem, their economies fall under judgment. America is now leading the world into a direct confrontation with God over Jerusalem. God's Word clearly says He will destroy the nations that come against Jerusalem!

December 1998

On Friday, December 11, 1998, the Judiciary Committee of the House of Representatives began to deliberate articles of impeachment against President Clinton. On December 12, the committee completed the deliberation and voted to approve four Articles of Impeachment against the president. The committee then forwarded the articles to the House for a vote on impeachment.

What was truly amazing, as the committee was voting on the four Articles of Impeachment, President Clinton was landing in the Palestinian controlled section of Israel! He agreed in October to come to Israel to insure the Wye agreement moved forward, and the timing was such that it occurred at the exact time Articles of Impeachment were drawn against him! Literally as he was landing in Israel the four Article of Impeachment was being drawn against him! On December 11 the headline articles of major newspapers had the impeachment and Clinton going to Israel on the front page. The radio and television news stories had the stories back to back. The Associated Press reported that the President went to Israel, **"Under an impeachment**

cloud." The Articles of Impeachment and Clinton's Mideast trip were tied together by every type of media. No one
following news could miss that the Articles of Impeachment charges against Clinton were completed while he was
in Israel forcing the Jews to give away the covenant land!
The news sources reported that the president was the
first in U.S. history to visit a Palestinian-ruled territory, and
that his visit was giving statehood status to the Palestinians. The capital of this state is to be Jerusalem! These same
news sources reported that Clinton was the first president
in one hundred thirty years to be impeached!

On December 15, President Clinton returned to Washington. Just four days later, the House of Representatives
voted to accept two of the Articles of Impeachment against
the president. The articles were then sent to the Senate for
a trial and upon conviction the president would be removed
from office.

I watched the political pundits who were astonished
that the House voted for impeachment. The various pundits said that up to two weeks before the impeachment it
was clear the House did not have the votes to impeach. The
pundits said that in the last two weeks many congressmen
became enraged with the president over this. Just before
the president left for Israel, he made a public speech about
the impeachment which further enraged the congressmen.
I thought back and two weeks before the impeachment vote
was when Arafat came to Washington and Clinton promised to give him $300-500 million in support. The presi-
dent had forty-two other countries agree to raise a total of
$3 billion for Arafat. At this exact time, the hearts of many
congressmen were turning against the president and for
impeachment!

God's Word is crystal clear that all who come against
God's covenant land and especially Jerusalem will be de-

stroyed. At every turn of the impeachment of the president had been his forcing the Jewish people to give away the covenant land.

March 1999

On March 23, Yasser Arafat met with President Clinton in Washington, D.C., to discuss a Palestinian state with Jerusalem as its capital. On March 24, Arafat went to the United Nations to discuss Palestinian statehood. On March 23, the stock market took the biggest fall in months. The market fell 219 points while Arafat was meeting with Clinton to carve up the nation of Israel.

On March 24 President Clinton authorized the attack on Serbia. The top military leaders in Russia made statements that World War III had begun. Viktor Chechevatov, a three-star general and commander of ground forces in Russia's Far East region, said this attack "was the beginning of World War III." Russia called for the draft of two hundred thousand soldiers, mobilized its fleet, and sent them into war maneuvers. During the maneuvers, Russia actually sent its bombers on a mock attack mission against America. The bombers were intercepted near Iceland and turned away from the route to America. Russia began to redeploy its tactical nuclear weapons. Russia had threatened NATO and America that the bombing of Serbia could lead to direct conflict with Russia.

The backdrop of the attack of Serbia was massive homosexual political activity across the entire fifty states and Arafat meeting with Clinton to carve up Israel. On June 9, 1999, Serbia withdrew it forces from Kosovo and the tension over Serbia subsided.

The long-term effect of this attack on Serbia was that hostile relations developed between America and both Russia and China. Russia and China entered into a military alliance. Russia supplied China with some of its best naval vessels and attack aircraft. China became very aggressive in its threats against America. The attack on Serbia has changed the entire course of world diplomacy. It is the opinion of this author that the attack on Serbia in the long run will be seen as the event which changed the long-term stability of the world. Only time will tell if this event will lead to a confrontation between the nations.

May 1999

On May 3, 1999, starting at 4:47 p.m. (Central Standard Time) the most powerful tornado storms to ever hit the United States fell on Oklahoma and Kansas. The wind of one tornado was officially measured at 316 mph, making it the fastest wind ever recorded. This tornado was very near to being classified as an F-6 on the tornado rating scale. There has never been an F-6 tornado.

The storm included many F-4 and F-5 tornadoes (F-5 have winds over 260 mph) which are extremely rare. There were almost fifty confirmed tornadoes, with nearly two hundred warnings! One F-5 tornado was over a mile wide and traveled for four hours, covering eighty miles on the ground. It destroyed everything in its path. This tornado was unprecedented in the history of tornadoes. F-5s make up less than one percent of all tornadoes. Tornadoes are usually a couple of hundred yards wide at the most, not over a mile; they seldom last for more than ten to fifteen minutes, not for four hours; and they usually stay on the ground for a couple of minutes, not four hours.

The damage of this storm was incredible. The headlines of the newspapers stated: "Everything was gone—At least 43 dead in monstrous Plains tornadoes;" "20 hours of terror:" "Stark scene: Miles of devastation;" "Tornadoes shred state." The National Oceanic and Atmospheric Administration stated, "This is an outbreak of historic proportions, no doubt about it." Oklahoma governor Frank Keating said, "This is the most calamitous storm we've ever seen and probably one of the more calamitous that ever hit the interior of the United States."

In Oklahoma City alone, more than two thousand homes were destroyed. Entire small communities disappeared as everything in the towns were leveled. The town of Mulhall, Oklahoma, ceased to exist. Thousands of automobiles and vehicles were destroyed. The total of the damage was in the billions of dollars. On May 4, parts of the states of Oklahoma and Kansas were declared federal disasters areas.

The storm warnings began at 4:47 p.m. (CST). In Israel, this would haven been 1:00 a.m. on May 4. May 4 was the date Yasser Arafat was scheduled to declare a Palestinian state with Jerusalem as its capital. This declaration was postponed until December 1999 at the request of President Clinton. President Clinton has already stated the Palestinian's should have their own state, that Jerusalem was negotiable, and he even refused to move the United States embassy to Jerusalem.

On May 4, President Clinton declared parts of Oklahoma and Kansas disaster areas. On this very same day, the president sent a letter to Arafat. In the letter Clinton, encouraged Arafat's aspirations for his "own land." The president said the Palestinians had a right to "determine their own future on their own land," and the Palestinians deserved "to live free, today, tomorrow and forever."

What an awesome warning to America. The most powerful tornadoes to **ever** hit the United States fell the same day (May 4, Israeli time) that Arafat was to proclaim a Palestinian state with Jerusalem as its capital. The United States has forced Israel into this "peace process," and pressured Israel to already give away some of the covenant land.

President Clinton had been the major force supporting Arafat. The very same day Clinton encouraged Arafat about the Palestinian state, he declared parts of America a disaster area from the worst tornadoes in history.

It appears, the rebellion of the American people against God is very soon coming to a climax. If America continues to pressure Israel to give away the covenant land and encourage Arafat, these types disasters and even greater can be expected. The disasters could be on a magnitude **never** before seen in our nation. The declaration of a Palestinian state with Jerusalem as its capital, backed by the government of the United States could release the dreaded wrath of the holy God of Israel on our nation.

September 1999

In late August, Hurricane Dennis began to affect the East Coast. This hurricane moved very slowly up the coast, drenching the states of Florida, Georgia, South and North Carolina. This was not a powerful hurricane, being listed as only a Category 2 with sustained winds of 105 mph. Although this hurricane was not powerful, it had tremendous rainfall.

Hurricane Dennis slowly moved up the coast and then stopped directly east of the Outer Banks of North Carolina. Dennis began to act very strangely. After stalling off North Carolina, it actually started backward along the course it came. Then the hurricane reversed itself and came back along the same course. It then stalled again off the Outer Banks and began to drift eastward. Finally, on September 3, after five straight days of lingering off the coast, Dennis struck North Carolina. Dennis' winds diminished quickly and did not cause tremendous damage. Dennis dropped tremendous amounts of rain and flooding occurred.

On September 1, Secretary of State Madeleine Albright

flew to the Middle East. Albright met with several Arab leaders before meeting with Yasser Arafat and Israeli prime minister Ehud Barak on September 3. The purpose of Albright's visit was to restart the Wye agreement which had stalled. This agreement, reached in October 1998, involved Israel giving away land for peace. As a result of this meeting between Albright, Arafat, and Barak, the talks were restarted and both sides agreed to have the final agreement for Israel to give land for peace by September 12, 2000. Both sides agreed to meet on September 13, 1999, to begin the final talks which would be concluded by September 2000.

Hurricane Dennis lingered off the coast of North Carolina nearly a week. The hurricane traveled in a bizarre path. At one point it actually reversed itself, and at another time was **heading away** from the coast. At nearly the exact time, Albright met in Israel, using the power of the United States to assist in Israel giving away the covenant land, Hurricane Dennis came ashore! This hurricane was literally doing circles in the Atlantic Ocean until the meeting in Israel. On this very day, the hurricane then hit the United States. Remember, this hurricane did not do tremendous damage, but it did drop enormous amounts of rain. This would prove to be extremely important just two weeks later when Hurricane Floyd hit.

On September 13, 1999, the Israeli foreign minister and one of Arafat's deputies met to work out arrangements for what is called the "final status" of Israeli giving land away. This meeting was a result of Albright's trip the week before. They agreed that by February 15, 2000, they would be able to present outlines for the borders of the Palestinian state, the status of Jerusalem, and the Jewish settlements in the West Bank and Gaza Strip.

On September 13, 1999, Hurricane Floyd strengthened

into a very dangerous Category 5 storm with sustained winds of 155 mph. The forecasters at the National Hurricane Center were astonished at how quickly Floyd grew in size and strength in one day. The actual statement was, **"Floyd grew unexpectedly into a monster of a storm on Sunday."** This was the very day the meeting was taking place in Israel to give away the land.

On September 16, Hurricane Floyd slammed into North Carolina. Floyd's winds had diminished to 105 mph, which was a Category 2, but this hurricane was huge in size. Hurricane force winds extended 150 miles in front of it. This hurricane caused the greatest evacuation in the history of the United States. As the storm moved up the coast, literally millions of people were evacuated in front of it.

The awesome destructive force of this storm was the rains. Rains of twenty inches or more fell over the entire eastern part of North Carolina. The rivers were still swollen and the land soaked from Hurricane Dennis which had hit just two weeks before. The destruction of this storm was awesome. The entire eastern section of the state, some eighteen thousand square miles, was destroyed.

In North Carolina, twenty-eight counties declared a state of emergency. Some four to five hundred roads were closed. Farmers estimated over 100,000 hogs; 2.47 million chickens and over 500,000 turkeys were dead. Huge amounts of horses and cattle also died. Sewage and water systems were knocked out. Sewage, chemicals, and dead animals all flowed into the rivers, creating an environmental nightmare. Some entire counties were nearly totally destroyed. The damage to agriculture was estimated at $1 billion. The loss to buildings, homes, and roads was in the billions. This was the greatest disaster to hit North Carolina since the Civil War.

While Israel was meeting with Palestine to give away

the covenant land, almost the entire East Coast of America was being ravaged by a monster hurricane. This hurricane grew into a monster the very day of the first meeting to reach the "final status" in the Middle East peace accord. This meeting was set by Secretary of State Albright just one week earlier! The land of Israel was being torn by pressure from the United States, and at the exact time the land of America was being ravaged by awesome destruction!

On September 21, the Dow Jones industrial average fell 225 points for the steepest loss in four months. On September 22, the stock market lost 74 points, and the next day, September 23, the market fell 205 points. The total loss for the three days was 504 points. This was the first time in the history of the stock market it suffered two 200 points losses during the same week! What was amazing about the loss was that it coincided exactly with Arafat visiting President Clinton to discuss the Wye agreement.

They met on September 22, the day between the two 200-point losses on the stock market! Arafat then left Clinton and went to the United Nations. There, he asked the U.N. to back independence for a Palestinian state. The stock market dropped 524 points for the week that Arafat came to discuss the Wye agreement and visit the U.N.

September witnessed some of the greatest destruction in United States history. This coincided exactly as the plan by President Clinton to have Israel give away the covenant land was being implemented. Arafat came and met with the president, and at that exact time the stock market had record losses.

October 1999

During the week of October 11, Jewish settlers on fifteen West Bank hilltops in Israel were evicted. This eviction was resisted by the settlers and the confrontation was reported in the national media during the week. Remember, President Clinton was the power behind Israel giving land for peace. On October 16, the *New York Times* ran a front-page article about this confrontation titled "On the West Bank, a Mellow View of Eviction." What is amazing, also on the front page was an article titled "Big Sell-Off Caps Dow's Worst Week Since October '89." During the week, the market lost 5.7 percent—the worst week since October 1989.

While Israel was forcing the settlers off the covenant land, the stock market was melting down. On October 15, the market lost 266 points! Also on October 15, Hurricane Irene hit North Carolina, and on the morning of the sixteenth, a powerful 7.1 earthquake rocked the Southwest.

On October 16, the fifth most powerful earthquake to hit America in the twentieth century struck California. The earthquake, named the Hector Mine, was 7.1 in magnitude and was located in the desert in a sparsely populated area. The earthquake did little damage, but shook three states. The earthquake was so powerful that it tore a twenty-five–mile gash in the earth. Millions of people in California, Nevada, and Arizona felt the power of the quake. This quake triggered small quakes near the San Andreas fault, which was one hundred twenty miles away. Seismologists referred to this as "nerve-rattling conversation" between the two fault lines. Earthquakes as powerful as 4.0 occurred a few miles from the San Andreas fault.

In a twelve-hour span, the stock market dropped 266 points, a hurricane hit the East Coast, and the West Coast was rocked by a huge earthquake. This all occurred as Jewish settlers were being evicted from the covenant land!

January 2000

On January 3, 2000, President Clinton met with Ehud Barak, Israeli prime minister, and Farouk al-Shara, the foreign minister of Syria. They met to discuss peace between Israel and Syria. This peace plan was for Israel to give back the Golan Heights. The Golan Heights is critical to the defense of Israel. When Syria controlled the Golan Heights, it was used as a position for the artillery to fire into Israel. The talks were to last two days, January 3 and 4, 2000.

On January 4, Israel's prime minister agreed to hand over five percent of its territory to the Palestinians, and the transfer was to be completed by the end of the week. The hand-over of this land came from previous agreements brokered by President Clinton.

By December 31, 1999, the stock market had reached its all-time high. On January 4, 2000, the stock market plummeted. Both the Dow and Nasdaq plunged. The Dow fell 359 points for the fourth worst one-day decline, and the Nasdaq fell 229 points for the worst drop ever. The combined losses in money for the one day was $600 billion. For the days of the meetings to pressure Israel to give away the covenant land, the stock market was reeling with losses.

When the meetings were completed, the market recovered the losses and it went on to register huge gains. The *New York Times* reflected on the stock market activity for the week with an article titled "The 3 U.S. Stock Gauges Rally to End a Turbulent Week." The turbulent week on Wall Street occurred exactly as the meeting was taking place to have Israel give away the Golan Heights and Israel agreed to give away five percent more of the West Bank.

March 10, 2000

On March 10, a milestone was reached when for the first time Israel offered the Palestinian's a state. Prime Minister Ehud Barak had just finished a two-day meeting with Arafat. The result was Israel was ready to offer about fifty percent of the West Bank (Judea-Samaria) as a Palestinian state.

The rest of the land would be negotiated at a later time. The issue of Jerusalem and Palestinian refugees was put off for a later date. Israel planned to annex about ten percent of the West Bank where the Jewish settlements are located. Barak wanted this all finished by September 13, 2000, when the seven years of the Oslo accords would have expired.

On March 10, the Nasdaq stock market index reached its high-water mark. The Nasdaq reached an all-time high of 5,048.62. Soon after this, the Nasdaq went into convulsions and would lose 3,500 points in a short time. This loss translated to trillions of dollars.

Remember, the United States was the force behind Israel offering its covenant land for peace. The very day Israel first offered a Palestinian state was the very high point of the Nasdaq, and since this day the Nasdaq has been in turmoil. Some of the greatest losses in the Nasdaq's history would occur on days directly related to U.S. involvement in Israel giving up the covenant land for "peace." This could be dramatically seen in the events of April 2000.

In April, President Clinton summoned Israel's prime minister Ehud Barak to Washington, D.C., for a conference regarding the peace process. They met on April 12. During the meeting, Clinton said that he wanted to get more involved with the peace process. This process involved Israel giving away the covenant land and possibly the dividing of Jerusalem. Barak agreed to Clinton's request.

On April 11–13, the Nasdaq section of the stock market collapsed. For these three days, the market fell over 600 points. The Nasdaq is the technical stocks, and in the 1990s it had grown $4 trillion dollars in value. For this week, the Nasdaq fell 618 points for the worst week ever.

At the precise time that Israel's prime minister was in Washington to meet with Clinton, the stock market was collapsing into the Nasdaq's worst week in its history. There is an apparent connection between Barak and Arafat coming to America to discuss the peace process and huge convulsions in the stock market. Could the stock market totally collapse someday, at the precise time Israel is being forced to divide the land or Jerusalem?

On June 16, 2000, President Clinton met with Yasser Arafat in the White House. They met to discuss the negotiations with Israel which had stalled. President Clinton made the statement that "I want to finish the job" with the peace process between Israel and the Palestinians. While in Washington, Arafat said that on September 13, 2000, a Palestinian state will be declared.

On this date the stock market fell 265 points. The market collapsed in the final hour of trading and had the lowest closing in months.

July–August 2000

Starting on July 12, 2000, President Clinton, Israeli prime minister Ehud Barak and Palestinian leader Yasser Arafat met at Camp David, Maryland, to try and reach an agreement for peace. The talks continued until July 26, when they collapsed. The talks collapsed over Jerusalem. President Clinton personally was involved in trying to divide Jerusalem into Muslim and Jewish sections. The talks also involved giving away huge sections of land to Palestinian control, which the president supported. No agreement was reached. Statements were made by Arafat that a Palestinian state was going to be declared with or without an agreement. Tension became very high after the meeting.

As the meeting was taking place, tremendous forest fires began to erupt in the West. The fires exploded in intensity at the end of July and then burned out of control during August. By the end of August, the fires had burned nearly seven million acres and were reported as some of the worst of the century. The states of Montana and Wyoming were declared a disaster area. There was no hope of putting the fires out; only the winter snows and rains could do it. All the forest firefighters in America were fighting these fires. The Army and National Guard were called to help fight the fires. Firefighters came from all over the world to help. More than twenty-five thousand were battling the fires.

Agriculture Secretary Dan Glickman reported the weather patterns over the western section of America were ideal for the fires and were like the events that created the Perfect Storm. There were high temperatures, low humidity, lightning storms with no rain, and high winds. This pattern lasted for months on end.

During the month of July the rains stopped in Texas. On July 28, Governor George Bush declared the state a disaster area for one hundred ninety-five counties because of the drought and fires. The state also went through the entire month of August without rain. The drought of over sixty days was compared to the one which caused the Dust Bowl of 1934. The drought of July-August 2000 was the worst in the state's history. While the meetings were taking place in America to partition Jerusalem and the covenant land of Israel, record-breaking droughts and forest fires were occurring. Entire states were declared disaster areas.

September–December 2000

On September 28, 2000, which was Rosh Hashana, the Jewish New Year, Ariel Sharon, the famous Israeli general, went to the Temple Mount in Jerusalem. The visit sparked rioting. The rioting continued unabated and escalated into a low-grade war. The riots resulted in hundreds of Jews being killed, and into the thousands of Palestinians. The rioting was attributed to the failed Camp David meetings in

July 2000. During these meetings, President Clinton had pressured Israel to give away large areas of Jewish settlements and sections of East Jerusalem. The sections of Jerusalem included the Temple Mount. The failure of the Camp David meeting destabilized the political situation between the Israelis and Palestinians.

By the end of October 2000, Prime Minister Barak's government had collapsed and Israel was without a government. In the face of the rioting, public support eroded and the Barak government collapsed. Israel had no government! On December 9, 2000, Barak resigned his position as prime minister and called for new elections. The elections were set for February 2001. The political situation in Israel immediately stabilized when Barak resigned and elections were set. From the end of October to December 9, Israel was in political chaos.

The United States held its presidential election on November 7. The election resulted in total political chaos, as neither candidate was declared a winner. The state of Florida hung in the balance to determine who would be elected president. The election dragged on and on until the Florida results went to the United States Supreme Court. On December 12, 2000, the court ruled and George W. Bush was declared the winner. From November 7 until December 12, the U.S. government was in chaos. There was no elected government.

The Israeli government was destabilized by the direct actions of President Clinton. Almost during the exact time the Israeli government was in chaos, the U.S. government was destabilized and in chaos. On December 9, when the election was set in Israel, a few days later the U.S. election was settled. Both governments were in chaos at nearly the exact time! What happened to the Israeli government, happened at the same time to the U.S. government. The country that was responsible for destabilizing Israel was itself destabilized at the very same time!

The U.S. presidential election was in total chaos. The election was held on November 7. President Clinton invited Arafat to Washington to try and renew the peace talks. The peace talks had completely broken down after the Camp David failure in July 2000 and the riots which started in September. Arafat arrived in Washington on November 9, as the U.S. was in the worst presidential crisis in over one hundred years! Arafat met with President Clinton just two days after the election while the election process was melting down! On November 9, the media headlines were the political crisis and Arafat meeting with Clinton!

June 2001

June 8 to June 9, 2001, saw one of the greatest rainfalls in the history of the United States in eastern Texas. In a twenty-four–hour period, over twenty-eight inches of rain fell in the Houston area. In fact, between June 5 and 11, three feet of rain fell on the area.

The rain was the product of Tropical Storm Allison, whose ten-day history will go down in Weather Bureau records as "weird." Allison formed within one day in the Gulf of Mexico, which is unusual in itself. This storm then headed into Texas east of Houston and broke up as a storm system. The remnants drifted to the north of Houston and circled around the city before sliding back south to the Gulf. The storm then re-formed into a tropical storm, which began to unleash incredible torrents of rain starting the evening of June 8 and continuing the next day.

The destruction in Houston alone was catastrophic. An estimated twenty-five thousand homes and businesses were destroyed or damaged, along with possibly fifty thousand automobiles and trucks. The city was closed for three days.

Twenty-eight counties in Texas were declared a disaster area, along with fourteen parishes in Louisiana. The resulting damage was close to $3 billion in Houston and $4 billion in the state. This was an incredible storm that did tremendous damage to southeast Texas. The storm then went into Florida and up the East Coast. Disaster areas were declared all the way to Pennsylvania. Meteorologists claim that Allison was the worst tropical storm in history. In the ten-day life of this storm, it unleashed enough rain for the entire United States for a year!

Texas is President Bush's home state. He was vacationing at his ranch in Crawford, Texas, at the time of the flooding. He declared the twenty-eight counties in Texas a federal disaster area while he was in Texas.

On June 6, President Bush sent CIA director George Tenet to Israel to try and broker a cease-fire between the Israelis and the Palestinians and to implement the Mitchell Report. This was the Bush administration's first real involvement in the Middle East crisis. Tenet wanted Israel to stop building in the settlement areas.

Tenet arrived in the Middle East on June 6. On June 8, the Central Intelligence Agency director hosted talks between senior Israeli and Palestinian security officials, while assistant Secretary of State William Burns met Palestinian president Yasser Arafat. This was at the same time Allison re-formed as a tropical storm and began dumping this tremendous rain. The two events exactly coincided! On the nightly news, the Houston flooding and the meetings in Israel were reported together! This tropical storm ravaged the United States for the entire time the CIA director was in Israel.

The massive destruction by Allison and the intervention by the CIA director were both major front-page headlines in the June 13, 2001, issue of the *New York Times*. One article was titled "Flood Tunneled into Houston's Cultural Heart." The second was titled "Two Sides in Mideast Accept U.S. Plan For a Cease-Fire."

God's Perfect Storm Warnings

The last three presidents have all been personally touched at the exact time they were involved with forcing Israel over the covenant land. Each president has been given what appears as a "Perfect Storm Warning."

The destruction by Tropical Storm Allison marked the third time since the Madrid peace process began in 1991 that a sitting president's home state had been the location of a powerful and damaging storm. These powerful storms occurred at the exact time the presidents were involved with Israel over the covenant land.

The first disaster literally destroyed President George H. Bush's home in Maine. This storm, which came to be known as "the Perfect Storm," happened while President Bush was initiating the Madrid peace process on October 31, 1991.

According to meteorologists, a "perfect storm" occurs once every one hundred years. The "Perfect Storm" formed in the North Atlantic and headed west for one thousand miles. The normal weather patterns in the United States are west to east, not east to west. This was one of the most powerful storms ever. It generated waves over one hundred feet high, the highest ever reported in the North Atlantic Ocean. As the storm moved west, it sent thirty-foot waves smashing against President Bush's summer home in Maine. The storm actually struck while the president was opening the Madrid peace process. When the president returned home, he had to go to Maine to oversee the repair of his home.

In March of 1997, President Clinton invited Palestinian leader Yasser Arafat to the White House to discuss "problems" with Jerusalem. While Arafat was en route, a powerful tornado storm ripped through seven states, with the worst damage in Arkansas, Kentucky, and Ohio. This was one of the most powerful tornado storms ever.

Clinton's home state of Arkansas bore the brunt of the storm, with thirteen counties declared a disaster area. This storm brought record flooding to the Ohio River. Clinton met with Arafat, and the headline of a *New York Times* front-page article on March 4, 1997, read "President Clinton Rebukes Israel." The headline of the adjacent article read "In Storms' Wake: Grief And Shock." The report of Clinton's home state being devastated by tornadoes was on the front page of the *New York Times* right next to the one of Clinton verbally rebuking Israel.

The home states of all three of these presidents were affected by severe weather patterns simultaneously to their diplomatic dealings with Israel. All this diplomatic dealing involved putting pressure on Israel over the covenant land.

The enormous damage to President George H. Bush's home in Maine by "the Perfect Storm" was eerie, coming just as he was directly responsible for initiating the Madrid Peace Process. What is also strange is the official residence of President George Bush, Sr., is in Houston, Texas. President Bush Sr. initiated the "peace process" and the very first time his son, as president, became involved in the "peace process" George Bush, Sr.'s home city was devastated by another freakish storm!

All three of these storms were ferocious and record-breaking. Both George W. Bush and Clinton had to declare disaster areas in their own states at the very time they were dealing with Israel. Look at the devastation that has hit home to each president as they have touched "the apple of God's eye" Israel.

A clear pattern of warnings has now developed. Are these presidents being warned by God not to interfere with the covenant land of Israel? Can all of this just be a coincidence? Or has God signaled a "perfect storm warning" to each president and to the nation?

September 11, 2001

On September 11, the greatest attack ever on American soil occurred. The hijacking of four airplanes and the attack on the World Trade Center (WTC) in New York City and the Pentagon in Washington, D.C., left upward of thirty-five hundred dead. These suicide attacks by Muslim terrorists caused approximately $40 billion in damage and stunned the country. On this day, America had come under the attack of terrorism on a scale not imagined. More Americans died on September 11, than on the attack on Pearl Harbor or the D-Day invasion. The attack was a complete surprise and came without any warning.

The attack on the WTC was at the very heart of the United States financial center. The largest stock brokerage firms in the world were in the WTC, along with many of the international banks. The attack was aimed right at the financial heart of the United States. The effect of this attack on the stock market was devastating. The week after the attack was one of the worst ever for the stock market. It may be the catalyst for an economic depression that could affect the entire world.

On August 9, 2001, a suicide terrorist killed nineteen Jews and wounded over one hundred people in a Jerusalem pizzeria. Later on that day, President Bush made a speech condemning the terrorist attack. After condemning the attack, the president then demanded that Israel abide by the Madrid peace process, the Mitchell Plan, and United Nations Resolutions 242 and 338. An excerpt of the

President's speech follows:

> The United States remains committed to implementa-
> tion, in all its elements, of the Mitchell Committee Re-
> port, which provides a path to return to peace negotia-
> tions based on United Nations Security Council Resolu-
> tions 242, 338 and the Madrid Conference. To get to
> Mitchell, the parties need to resume effective security
> cooperation and work together to stop terrorism and vio-
> lence.

These U.N. resolutions called for Israel to go back to the borders prior to the Six-day War of 1967. These U.N. resolutions would require Israel to give up East Jerusalem, the Golan Heights, and end all settlements on the West Bank. The president was totally ignoring the covenant Israel has with God. He was telling Israel to go back to borders that were indefensible, thus putting Israel in a very dangerous position. The president ended the speech by telling Israel to negotiate with the very people who had just committed a horrible terrorist attack.

On October 2, 2001, the major news sources reported that at the time of the attack on 9/11, the U.S. government was in the process of recognizing a Palestinian state. Just prior to September 11, the Bush administration had formulated a policy of recognizing a Palestinian state with East Jerusalem as its capital. The secretary of state, on September 13, was going to notify the Saudi Arabian ambassador of this plan. The plan was going to be announced by the secretary of state at the U.N. General Assembly on September 23. The attack on September 11 derailed this plan. At the very time the U.S. was going to force Israel into coexistence with terrorist that were dedicated to the destruction of the Jewish nation, the U.S. came under attack by the same terrorists!

Since September 2000, Israel was the subject of continued terrorist attacks and hundreds of Jews had been killed by the terrorists. Israel was engaged in a low-grade war being waged by the Palestinians. In the face of the terrorism and war, President Bush wanted Israel to negotiate with the Palestinians and give away the covenant land, including East Jerusalem.

Exactly thirty-two days later, the Muslim terrorists struck America. America now had come under the same type of terror that the Israelis were under. America was heading into war against Muslim terrorists just like Israel was engaged in. Israel was fighting for its very existence and now America was in the same battle for existence.

In October 1991, America had forced Israel into the Madrid peace process. This process reached a climax in July 2000 with Israel offering to give up East Jerusalem and most of the West Bank. This offer failed. The Palestinians then started the war using intense terrorism against Israel. Israel was politically destabilized, and its economy greatly suffered.

As America has forced Israel to give up sections of the covenant land, the identical pressure has come upon America. The parallel between what happened in Israel since September 2000 and now America is exactly the same. These are the parallels:

- At the same time the Israeli government was destabilized in late 2000, so was America's.
- Almost a year to the day that the intense terrorism began against Israel, America was attacked by the same type of terrorists.
- Jerusalem, the capital of Israel, was under terrorist attack and Washington, D.C., was also under attack by terrorists.

- Israel was in a low-grade war with Muslims. America also entered into a low-grade war with Muslims.
- Israel's capital, Jerusalem, was attacked by terrorists. America's capital, Washington, D.C., was also attacked by terrorists.
- Americans had come under the same fear that the Israelis live under.
- Israel's economy suffered because of the terrorism. The American economy fell under the same pressure.
- The tourist industry collapsed in Israel because of the terrorism. The tourism industry in America collapsed after the terrorist attacks.

The American policy since October 1991 had been to pressure Israel to give away the covenant land for "peace." This has resulted in America suffering in 2001 exactly as Israel. America had touched the "apple of God's eye" and paid an enormous price. God's Word says that what a nation does to Israel will come right back upon that nation. This can be plainly seen as what happened to the United States. The pressure from God will only get worse if America continues to force Israel over the covenant land.

> For the day of the LORD is near upon all the heathen: as thou hast done, it shall be done unto thee: thy reward shall return upon thine own head.
>
> —Obadiah 1:15

October 2001

On October 2, President Bush stated publicly for the first time that he was in favor of a Palestinian state, which included East Jerusalem as its capital. On the same day, the national anthrax terrorist attack began in Florida as one man contracted anthrax and died shortly thereafter. The man died on October 5. This began a growing spate of "anthrax anxiety," with findings in the offices of prominent government and media personalities.

Anthrax was a very rare occurrence before October 2. After October 2, the anthrax scare touched the entire nation. There were eighteen inhalant anthrax cases from 1900 to 1976, none from 1976 to 2001. The president's public announcement of his support for a Palestinian state coincided exactly with the anthrax terrorism outbreak.

November 2001

The United Nations meeting that was canceled because of the terrorist attack on the WTC was rescheduled for November 10, 2001. On November 10, President Bush addressed the U.N. and spoke mostly about terrorism. He did briefly speak about the Middle East and stated that there should be two states. There should be an Israel and Palestine. He called for the borders to be in accordance with Security Council resolutions 242 and 338. This means the dividing of Jerusalem and Israel giving away huge sections of the covenant land. The part of the president's speech touching on Israel follows:

> The American government also stands by its commitment to a just peace in the Middle East. We are working toward the day when two states—Israel and Palestine—live peacefully together within secure and recognized borders as called for by the Security Council resolutions.
>
> We will do all in our power to bring both parties back into negotiations. But peace will only come when all have sworn off forever incitement, violence and terrorism.

On November 11, Yasser Arafat spoke to the U.N. General Assembly. He also spoke about a Palestinian state and blamed Israel for all the fighting since September 2000. Later this day, Secretary of State Colin Powell met with Arafat.

Powell also made a public statement about Israel and a Palestinian state. He said, "Palestine entered the government's lexicon with President Bush's speech to the United Nations, another sign of the U.S. commitment to an eventual Palestinian state." He also said, "If one is moving forward with a vision of two states side by side, it's appropriate to all those states what they will be, Israel and Palestine. No Republican president has ever made such a statement."

On November 9, 2001, Osama bin Laden threatened the United States for the first time with nuclear and chemical weapons. On November 10, President Bush tried to downplay the threatening statements by Osama. On November 11, 2001, Saddam Hussein also threatened the U.S. with nuclear weapons. Secretary of Defense Rumsfeld said the threats were to be taken seriously. On November 14, Kabul was captured and some of Osama's records were found, including plans for building a nuclear bomb.

On November 12, 2001, an American Airlines jet crashed taking off from JFK Airport killing two hundred sixty-five people. This crash was less than twenty-four hours after Arafat's speech to the U.N. The speech was about fifteen miles from the crash scene in the very same city!

At the exact time the president was speaking to the U.N. about a Palestinian state, the U.S. for the first time was threatened by Osama bin Laden and Saddam Hussein with nuclear weapons. The very day the president addressed the U.N. he had to downplay the nuclear threats against America! Time will tell if the threats had any merit.

The Results of Meeting With Yasser Arafat

✦ September 1, 1993: President Clinton announces he will meet Arafat and Rabin on September 13 in Washington, D.C., to begin the Oslo peace accords. After nearly a week of meandering in the Atlantic Ocean, Hurricane Emily hits North Carolina on this day.

✦ March 2, 1997: Arafat meets with President Clinton in Washington, D.C. The same day, awesome tornado storms unleash tremendous damage in Arkansas and flooding in Kentucky and Ohio. Arkansas and Kentucky declared disaster areas.

✦ January 21, 1998: President Clinton is waiting to meet with Arafat at the White House. At this exact time, the president's sex scandal breaks.

✦ September 27, 1998: Arafat is meeting with the president in Washington. Hurricane Georges hits Alabama and stalls. The hurricane stalls until Arafat leaves and then it dissipates. Parts of Alabama declared a disaster area.

✦ October 17, 1998: Arafat comes to the Wye Plantation meeting. Incredible rains fall on Texas, which cause record flooding. Parts of Texas are declared a disaster area.

✦ November 23, 1998: Arafat comes to America. He meets with President Clinton who is raising funds for the Palestinian state. On this day the stock market fell 216 points.

✦ December 12, 1998: On this day the U.S. House of Representatives votes to impeach President Clinton. At the very time of the impeachment, the president is meeting with Arafat in Gaza over the peace process.

✦ March 23, 1999: Arafat meets with Clinton in Washington, D.C. Market falls 219 points that day. The next day Clinton orders attack on Serbia.

• September 3, 1999: Secretary of State Albright meets with Arafat in Israel. Hurricane Dennis comes ashore on this very day after weeks of changing course in the Atlantic Ocean.

• September 22, 1999: Arafat meets with Clinton in Washington, D.C. The day before and after the meeting, the market falls more than 200 points each day. This was the first time in history the market lost more than 200 points for two days in a week. The market lost 524 points this week.

• June 16, 2000: Arafat meets with President Clinton. The market falls 265 points on this day.

• July 12–26, 2000: Arafat at the Camp David meetings. Powerful droughts throughout the country. Forest fires explode in West into uncontrolled fires. By the end of August, 7 million acres are burnt.

• November 9, 2000: Arafat meets with President Clinton at the White House to try and salvage the peace process. This was just two days after the presidential election. The nation was just entering into an election crisis which was the worst in over one hundred years.

• November 11, 2001: Arafat speaks at the U.N. General Assembly and condemns Israel. He later meets with Secretary of State Colin Powell. On this day, Saddam threatens the U.S. with nuclear weapons. Within twenty-four hours of meeting with Powell, an airplane crashes in NYC killing two hundred sixty-five people. The crash was fifteen miles from where Arafat spoke.

God has very clearly shown that America is on a collision course with Him over the land of Israel. President George

H. Bush was the initiator of the peace plan to give away the land of Israel. On the very day the meeting opened in 1991, a freakish storm originated in the North Atlantic Ocean and heavily damaged the president's home. President Bush's land was damaged. On the day the peace process moved to the United States, the nation's land was devastated by powerful Hurricane Andrew. This was the worst national disaster ever to hit America.

President Clinton met with President Assad of Syria, and he boldly said Israel had to give away the Golan Heights to Syria. Within twenty-four hours, the land of America was rocked by the powerful Northridge earthquake. President Clinton met with Arafat, and he publicly rebuked Israel. Within twenty-four hours, Arkansas, the president's homeland, was hit by devastating tornadoes. This tornado storm was one of the worst ever recorded. Arafat then tours America, and during the exact time of the tour some of the worst flooding hit the land of the Ohio Valley. At this same time, powerful snowstorms fell on the land of the North Plains, which eventually helped cause awesome floods.

In March and April 1997, the United Nations condemned Israel over Jerusalem. In July 1997, the U.N. called for a boycott of products coming from the land of Israel. In July 1997, an economic crisis started in Asia that touched the entire world. Billions of dollars were needed to try and stabilize these nations. Nations which economies seemed to be endlessly growing, overnight were reduced to poverty!

In September 1998, Arafat came to the United States to speak with President Clinton and address the United Nations. Arafat's objective was to force Israel to give away thirteen percent of the land and gain recognition of a Palestinian state with Jerusalem as the capital. The exact time Arafat was in the United States, Hurricane Georges slammed into the Gulf Coast causing over $1 billion in damage. At the very time Israel was politically destabilized, so was the United States during the election of 2000. The worst tropical storm ever coincided with diplomatic pressure on Israel over the settlements in the West Bank. The correlation between disasters hitting America and forcing Israel over the covenant land continued right into the summer of 2001.

God intends to keep His promise with Abraham and the Jewish people. God will let no nation, including the United States, stand in the way of fulfilling His promise. America is in an extremely dangerous position before the Lord God of Israel. God has a controversy with the nations over Jerusalem. "Behold, he that keepeth Israel shall neither slumber nor sleep" (Psalm 121:4).

Chapter 7
Palestinian Cause in Proper Perspective

Nearly every day now the media carries stories about Israel and the Palestinians. One of the major issues is Israel giving away some of the covenant land for peace. This land would include part of Jerusalem, which contains the section that includes the site of the ancient Temple. Israel has been forced to give land up for "peace" since the Balfour Declaration of 1917. Dr. Gary Frazier has written an excellent article on this topic. His article in part follows.

Dr. Gary Frazier of Discovery Ministries, Arlington, Texas, provides the following material from his booklet *In the Arab/Israeli Puzzle—Historical Fact vs. Fallacy.*

What Is the Issue

According to the Palestinians, the real issue is their desire to have a homeland, a state, in what is now Israel, and control over sites they consider holy in East Jerusalem. They say they want to have the land back that was supposedly taken from them in the Six-Day war of 1967. This certainly sounds reasonable enough. In fact, so much so that many Israelis support a peace agreement with these articles included in it. Having said this, is this really what the Palestinians want, or do they really want the extermination of Israel and control of all that we now know as Israel?

The hatred, anger, and violence against Jewish citizens expose the true objective. One objective they might try to achieve is a state. The true objective, they will never achieve. How can I say this with such certainty? Because God has said so! By the way, in case you have forgotten, Israel did not take the land from the Palestinians in 1967. No one ever mentions it, but Jordan, Syria, and Egypt controlled the land gained by Israel. The Palestinians were never in control of this territory. Therefore, if the land were to be given back, it would have to be returned to Jordan, Syria, and Egypt. However, I must say here, to show how the Israelis desired to foster good will after the Six-Day War, Israel gave control and stewardship of the Temple Mount area to the Muslims. General Moshe Dayan has yet to be forgiven by many Israelis for this act of wishful peaceful diplomacy.

The Truth About the Land

During the entire period of recorded history, that is more than 5,000 years, Palestinian Arabs never ruled Palestine. I want to repeat this due to the fact it is never spoken of by the media. The fact is the only constant presence in the land has been a Jewish presence since the birth of Isaac. The numbers of Jews may have been minute at times, but they have remained, regardless. In addition to the Jews, there have been the soldiers of the occupying forces and their slaves.

Century after century the culture, social fabric, and identity of these inhabitants changed as the ruling powers changed. Only the Jewish presence remained consistent as the sole survivors in the land, and they alone have maintained an uninterrupted national link since Abraham and Isaac.

In the current worldwide discussion regarding the

land of Israel, no one seems to mention the fact that the Jewish claim to the land goes back 4,000 years with centuries filled with vital and consistent national life supported by biblical and archaeological proofs. For 3,000 years Jerusalem was the capital of the Hebrew nation. The historical and archaeological evidence is irrefutable. King David legally purchased the 35-acre area known today as Temple Mount, currently said to be the center of the dispute, from Araunah the Jebusite (2 Samuel 24:21–24). This very piece of ground became the site of both the First and Second Temples in Israel; the center of Jewish life and identity 1700 years before anyone ever heard of the Dome of the Rock (687–691 A.D.), or the Al Aksa mosque.

Zechariah, as he unfolds the prophetic scenario of God's great deliverance of Israel at the end of the age, said, "In that day will I make the governors of Judah like an hearth of fire among the wood, and like a torch of fire in a sheaf; and they shall devour all the people round about, on the right hand and on the left: and Jerusalem shall be inhabited again in her own place, even in Jerusalem" (Zechariah 12:6). This last phrase in the original Hebrew text simply says that Jerusalem shall dwell where Jerusalem always was.

The Palestinian People

Though there were Arab communities scattered in the territory of biblical Israel during the last hundreds of years, there was never a nation called Palestine ruled by local peoples. So, who are the real Palestinians? History records that all the inhabitants of the land came to be known as Palestinians since this was the name of the territory and even the Jews were called Palestinians until 1948. In fact, the early Jewish pioneers who joined those already in the land at the turn of the 20th century later carried Palestinian identity cards issued by the British, circa 1918, as their provisional passports. This was done until 1948 when all residents in the area became Israeli citizens, both Jews and Arabs.

It is interesting that during WWII, the British army drafted and operated a Palestinian Brigade made up entirely of Jewish troops. The Palestinian Symphony was 100% Jewish, and the *Palestine Post* (later to become the *Jerusalem Post*) was an entirely Jewish newspaper. The point is this: being a Palestinian had no bearing regarding one's nationality, religion, or ethnic background. It merely pointed to the geographical location of one's residence and nothing more.

The current Palestinians are the descendants of Arabs who arrived in Palestine, for the most part, only in the last two hundred years. Why did they come from the Arab regions? The answer is economic. The Arabs flooded into Palestine seeking jobs provided by Jewish commercial developments, which began in the late 1800s.

The myth of a national Arab Palestine that goes back generations is a fantasy and a myth, as well as an outright lie. There are no historical facts to document these claims. I want to hasten to add there are some Arab clans who can trace roots back for many generations, but they represent only a small, small fraction of the Arab population of today.

Palestine was never an established Arab nation taken away by the Jewish Zionists. Let me repeat this, Palestine was never an established Arab nation taken away by the Jewish Zionists. The truth is the Arab families who came to work in the land never felt any political ties to the land because they had always existed under the occupation of some foreign power. It was for this reason, both the Balfour Declaration of 1917 and the League of Nations Mandate following WWI, charged the Jewish population in Palestine with guaranteeing the civil and religious rights of minorities in the land. These statements clearly recognized the only national claim to the land was that of the Jewish population.

In fact, the Arabs themselves, in the first quarter of the century, recognized the land as being the home for the Jews and expressed, in general, a very cordial acceptance. This was clearly demonstrated in the agreement of January 3, 1919, between Emir Feisal of Arabia and Dr. Chaim Weizmann, head of the World Zionist Organization. The Emir, a respected spokesman for the Arabs at the time, spoke with much favor regarding the future cooperation between the newly carved out Arab states and the future Jewish one. In Article 1 the Emir said, "The Arab states and Palestine (the Jewish State), in all their relations and undertakings, shall be controlled by the most cordial good will and understanding."

The Emir identified and welcomed the emergence of a Jewish nation in Palestine parallel to the emergence of Arab nations in the region such as Syria, Jordan, Lebanon, Iraq, Iran, etc., under both the British and French mandates. On March 3, 1919, in a letter to Felix Frankfurter, U.S. Supreme Court Justice, the Emir stated,

"The Arabs, especially the educated among us, look with deepest sympathy on the Zionist Movement. Our deputation here in Paris is fully acquainted with the proposals submitted yesterday by the Zionist Organization to the Peace Conference and we regard them as moderate and proper. We will do our best insofar as we are concerned to help their attainment; we will offer the Jews a hearty welcome home. . . . I think that neither can be a success without the other."

Unfortunately these sentiments did not last very long.

The Palestinian Refugee Problem

In 1947 the Arabs were offered their own state along-side the area being granted to Israel. The answer from the Muslim was, they would never live in peace with the Jews, and drive them all into the Mediterranean.

On May 15, 1948, just one day after Israel's Declaration of Independence, five Arab nations attacked the infant state. Bear in mind there were only 675,000 Jews in Israel versus more than 50 million Arab Muslims. The Muslim nations called for the Arab residents of the area to get out of the way in light of the coming invasion, promising them a quick defeat of the Jews and an opportunity to plunder Jewish property and homes following their victory. However, the Muslim world forgot one very essential element, they were not fighting the tiny Jewish state, they were fighting God himself who was in the process of keeping His Word spoken long ago by the ancient prophets.

After eight months of fighting, a cease-fire was established and the Arabs who fled could now no longer return to their willfully vacated property. Some were driven off by the Jews during the fighting. This was the beginning of the Palestinian refugee problem or the "Plight of the Palestinian" as so-called by the media. Following the War of Independence, Jordan took control over the region of Judea and Samaria on the West Bank of the Jordan River, which extends to Jerusalem. Egypt likewise controlled the Gaza Strip region as well as the Sinai Peninsula.

The Palestinian Arab population, many living in their own villages and some in U.N. constructed refugee camps, were under the authority of neighboring friendly

Arab Muslim countries. The irony of it was they were now in the very territory allotted to them as their state by U.N. resolution Number 181 of 1947, which had apportioned them a state next to the Jewish State. This was the very territory they had declined, preferring to have it all! It was not too late! At that time they could still have clamored for their own state but they did not. The question is why? Why did they not lay claim to the land as their state?

To understand this one must understand something of the Muslim mentality (I will say more about this later). Islam is a non-tolerant religion and cannot peacefully coexist with any other religion. Therefore, rather than live alongside a Jewish state in peace the Muslim nations chose to use the Palestinian people as pawns for sympathy, political manipulation and economic gain.

The neighboring Muslim countries elected to keep these people locked in a prison of dirty politics and abuse giving them no chance for economic gain, education, or a future with real hope. I repeat it was the Muslim nations who did this to their own people. Using them to deceive the world and pressure Israel into compromises. I personally viewed some of these refugee camps. The filth, squalor, and overall conditions were awful to say the least. The neighboring Muslim countries could have alleviated this suffering, had they so desired.

In June of 1967, Israel, learning of a certain attack upon her by her enemies, went to war after 19 years of continued skirmishes and acts of terrorism perpetrated against her by the Muslims. The result of the Six-Day War was Israel's gaining control of the Jordan Valley and the West Bank, the Old City of Jerusalem, the Golan Heights, Gaza Strip, and the Sinai. Israel increased her land mass from 8,000 square miles to 26,000 square miles. During the war, the refugees in the Jordan Valley fled across the Jordan River into Jordan and those in the Golan fled into Syria, with most in the Gaza Strip and Sinai fleeing to Egypt. Sad as it was, they were not welcomed and rather than being accepted became the lowest class among the people.

I personally feel great sorrow for the Palestinian Arabs. They have been fed a steady diet of hatred, anger, and vengeance. They have been told the Jews are responsible for their every problem and the answer is to kill as many as they can at all cost. The Muslim world operates on the same system as many historical revisionists in America today, and that is, if you tell a lie often enough it becomes true!

Palestinian Statehood

The world is clamoring today for a Palestinian state. What is incredible is that this myth has been and is being spread by people who should know better. It is incredible that this mythical state has already been recognized by the U.N. and given observer status. Amazingly this mythical state has a recognized president, Yasser Arafat (although never elected), and has been awarded ambassadorial status in several nations. In addition, many nations are pledging millions of dollars in financial support. Again, let me go back to 1947. Britain had made two sets of territorial promises during WWI. One promise to the Jews; a second to the Muslims.

The British sought to keep their promise to the Muslims while repeatedly violating the ones made to the Jews. It was clear to everyone the Arabs were being favored as nearly 20 new Arab states were carved out of the former Turkish Empire while at the same time the land mass promised to the Jews was being reduced dramatically.

Of the land originally promised to Israel, only one-fifth was actually given, while the other 78 percent was given to what is now Jordan. Yet, in spite of this obvious retraction of both Britain's promise and that of the League of Nations, the Israelis accepted this. Yet, in spite of Israel's willingness to accept this small portion, peace did not come and the Muslims attacked. However, the question begs to be asked, "Why did the British renege on their promise?" The answer is as follows. During the 1930s, as Adolf Hitler was coming into power in Germany, nearly 100,000 German Jews fled to what was then Palestine.

The Muslim population did not like this large influx of Jews and began murderous anti-Jewish campaigns lasting some three years. The British, anxious to gain the support of the Muslim population against the Nazis, stopped the Jewish immigration. Europe was killing them, America would take in a limited number, and now Palestine was closed to them as well. The Jewish leadership clamored for an end to this blockade into Palestine.

Due to the fact over six million Jews were slaughtered by the Nazis (a historical truth denied by some of the Muslims), the Jewish leaders demanded the end of the British Mandate and their own state. The Muslims likewise wanted the British out but instead demanded the entire area of Palestine to be one nation with an Arab majority. This matter was hotly debated in the newly formed United Nations and the vote was in favor of a Jewish state. However, there were numerous problems with the proposed territory since it comprised only 22% of the originally promised land. In addition, it was then partitioned into two states, one Jewish and one Arab.

The area to be Jewish was made up of three disconnected regions largely desert with over 600 miles of indefensible frontier. Biblical Judea, Samaria, Gaza, and much of the Galilee were taken away. The Old City of Jerusalem itself was to become an international city within the Palestinian state. As heartbreaking as this was to the Jewish people the leadership accepted this U.N. plan and on May 14, 1948, David Ben-Gurion read the Declaration of Independence of the new State of Israel. This compromise, this incredible concession still did not bring the desired peace.

The Arabs rejected the Partition Plan, demanding all the land. Therefore, on May 15 the armies of Lebanon, Jordan, Syria, Egypt, and Iraq, along with contingents of several other Muslim countries, attacked the one-day-old state. The Grand Mufti of Jerusalem, Yasser Arafat's uncle, was quoted as announcing, "I declare a Jihad (holy war), my Muslim brothers! Murder the Jews! Murder them all!"

History reveals this attempt by evil to annihilate the Jews failed. Remember: What God promises, God performs. God had promised a return to the land and because of this God was and is going to preserve the Jews in the land until Jesus comes! After nearly a year the war ended but without recognition on the part of the Muslim world of Işrael's right to be in the land. Jordan moved to annex Judea, Samaria, and east Jerusalem as its own.

The obvious result would be years of hatred with these areas becoming breeding grounds from which to launch terrorist attacks against Israeli citizens. The irony of this was that now instead of the Palestinians having their own state, the Jordanians and the Egyptians occupied and controlled the land that had been offered to them. The Palestinians were isolated in refugee camps and kept as a subjugated people by their very own relatives!

The "land for peace" formula has never worked and will never work! The true motivation behind the quest for a modern Palestinian state is the extermination of the Jews. If this were not true then answer this, "Why must the Muslims have this tiny piece of land, when there are 32 Muslim nations with a land mass of more than 672 times the size of Israel with unlimited oil reserves?" The Muslim nations are more than twice the size of America, while Israel would fit in the peninsula between Orlando and Miami, Florida. Another illustration is that Israel is no larger than the state of New Jersey. In spite of it all, the motivation is demonic and giving more land will not resolve nor end the conflict. By the way, it is hypocritical for America to insist the Jews give up their land, unless Americans are willing to give America back to the Indians.

Jerusalem

Jerusalem has been, is, and will continue to be the major stumbling block in any attempted peace. It should be noted and understood that Jerusalem was never an Arab Muslim or Palestinian capital. Jerusalem has been an occupied city since 63 B.C. Jerusalem was nothing more than a provincial city under foreign control that played practically no economic, social, or political role in the region since its destruction under Titus in A.D. 70. That having been stated, I must rush to add that Jerusalem is mentioned in the Bible more than 800 times and has been at the heart of Jewish life for more than 3,000 years. In contrast to this fact, Jerusalem is not mentioned even once in the Koran, the Muslim holy book. I repeat: the city of Jerusalem is not named even once in the Koran!

As to the idea of East Jerusalem being the capital of a Palestinian state, one must remember there was no East

Jerusalem until the Jordanians illegally annexed this area
in 1948 and drove all Jews out. In addition, the Muslims
began the process of systematically destroying all of the
Jewish and Christian holy sites, attempting to erase the
very roots of Jewish history for the last 3,000 years.

The Muslims speak often of their holy sites in Jerusalem. The fact is there are none! How then did Jerusalem
become the often stated third most holy city in Islam
after Mecca and Medina? In the Koran, Sura 17:1, it
speaks of Al Aksa which according to Alfred Guildaume,
a researcher of Islam, translates to, the farthest mosque,
and does not refer to Jerusalem but to a mosque in al-
Girana on the outskirts of Medina.

It should be noted that when this Sura was written
there was no mosque in Jerusalem on the Temple Mount
named Al Aksa or anything else. Supposedly, it was from
this distant place Mohammed ascended into heaven on
his winged horse, El Baruk. This story comes from the
17th Sura (this word means chapter and verse in the
Koran) and reads, "From the sacred temple to the temple
that is most remote, whose precinct we have blessed that
we might show him our signs."

As a result of this alleged event, Jerusalem and the
Temple Mount in particular have become holy to Islam.
However, bear in mind there is no more evidence supporting this story than there is that New York City was
the place! By the way, the Dome of the Rock, built by
Abd-al-Malik between A.D. 687 and 691 was built on the
location of the Jewish Temple. The Al Aksa mosque was
built by Caliph Walid, Malik's son, between 709 and 715,
and was built upon the foundation of a Byzantine church
and still follows the general lines of a basilica.

What's the point you ask? Simple, the Muslims have
no valid claim to any site in Jerusalem since both of the

places are located in place of ancient Jewish and Christian sites, which predate Islam hundreds of years. In addition it should be noted there is absolutely no historical evidence that Mohammed ever visited Jerusalem before his death in A.D. 632.

Chapter 8
The Ten-Year Peace Process

It is a sad irony that many in America believe that the United States has stood by Israel. In reality, this nation has led them to the edge of the abyss through the policies of the Bush (the elder) and the Clinton administrations. The past policies of the State Department and the White House have been designed to protect the flow of Middle East oil. This same concern has occupied President George W. Bush and his administration. Regardless of the intentions, bad or good, these American policies have put the "apple of God's eye" in harm's way.

The United States has put a noose around Israel's neck by sponsoring, or co-sponsoring, the Madrid, Oslo, Wye, and Camp David agreements. More recently, and still on the table, are the Tenet and the Mitchell plans. The United States' Middle Eastern policy evolving from these efforts has largely been designed around protecting the flow of oil from that region.

In this regard, Israel has been used as insurance, even though considered a major presence and an American ally, to keep a United States foothold in the Mideast. During the ten-year peace process, the U.S. taxpayers have paid out billions of dollars in aide to our so-called Arab "allies," who have all sided against Israel since her independence in 1948.

When one steps back from this scenario, however, one can observe that the oil issue has moved biblical prophetic matters to a closer fulfillment. In other words, God is in control, and His plans will play out to perfection.

The Middle East Reality

The United States has prospered in the past, in spite of her social condition, because this nation has been there to protect Israel, and because of her Christian heritage. However, if United States policy causes Israel to go to war, will the same fate happen to the United States? That question appears to have been answered on September 11, 2001.

If the United States had been unconditionally in favor of Israel all along—meaning that if anybody attacked Israel, the U.S. would respond—the country would be in a better position right now. One major by-product would have been the development of a national energy program, allowing America to be much less reliant on the unpredictable Muslim nations.

But then again, the Bible, has foretold all these current events, leading this world to the imminent completion of the church age and the coming reign of Jesus Christ.

Even the church today, struggling with the apostasy prophesied in the same Bible which they purport to follow, falls under the shadow. Most Catholics, Methodists, Presbyterians, Episcopalians, and other denominations believe that the church has replaced Israel, and they don't understand the importance of Israel. They casually regard the Bible as a book and do not treat it as the active **Word of God.**

Even the reform and conservative Jews, who have been involved in the peace talks, have stepped in, trying to come up with a "deal" in the pursuit of peace and security to make life better in Israel. They also tried to use the land (God's covenant land) and not the Lord to help resolve the problem.

The radical Muslim leaders have called upon and co-opted the peacemakers of the United Nations and the United States. These are the same Muslims who want to destroy the nation of Israel and drive its people into the Mediterranean Sea. The American administration has been warned about not participating in the Israeli land giveaway through letters, books, and other published material. Unfortunately, attitudes and commitments have come so far that it is not easy to turn back. If the U.S. did change policy direction, it would greatly complicate political matters, but it would be a courageous, faith-led decision. Unfortunately, this scenario doesn't appear likely.

The Lord Is the Director

Many believed initially that some land would have to be given up by Israel as a part of the seven-year Oslo accords, thinking that it would become part of the Daniel 9:27 peace covenant that is prophesied to fail. However, history will record a different sequence of events.

Palestinian Authority chairman Yasser Arafat threw away the chance for Palestinian statehood, ninety-five percent of the West Bank, East Jerusalem, and peace in the Middle East, after the Camp David talks. Arafat declined all of this generous offer by Israeli prime minister Ehud Barak because he wanted sovereign control over the Temple Mount and the neighboring holy sites in East Jerusalem. Since that time, for whatever Arafat's reasoning might have been, there has been an escalation of conflict (the *intifada*) and more bloodshed for all the involved parties in the Middle East.

At about the same time, Syria's president Hafez el-Assad turned down Israel's offer of the Golan Heights because it did not include a one hundred-meter strip of land along the eastern shoreline of the Sea of Galilee. Today, both the Palestinians and the Syrians have very little to show for their efforts, and they will never see again what they once had on the table.

The Lord has used this long and drawn-out peace process to show:

- that none of Israel's land is not to be given up for peace.
- how important the Israeli settlements are to Him.
- how unreasonable the Palestinian and Syrian leaders had been.
- how the motives of the United Nations and their resolutions reflect partiality to the fifty-two Muslim member states, representing 1.2 billion people, and the importance of their oil.
- how the American government's economic interest in standing by Arab nations has been to protect Middle East oil.
- how some American churches lack knowledge regarding the significance of Israel and her covenant land.
- that the Catholic Church's complicity in the Vatican–Palestinian agreement of February 2000 is calling for Jerusalem to become an international city.
- that Pope John-Paul II's statements about lasting peace and about the "need" for all participants to fulfill the U.N. resolutions pertaining to Israel's covenant land reveal his lack of scriptural significance.

This ten-year process revealed much to those with eyes to see and ears to hear. However, the days ahead will be even more significant.

The Middle East Stage

In effect, both the Palestinians and the Syrians blew their opportunities, and now they are dealing with the much tougher government of Prime Minister Ariel Sharon. The majority of the people of Israel were tired of the frustrating peace process, and the result was the election of Sharon by a landslide.

In reality, however, the peace process is not just about the land. It is about an ancient conflict between two faiths, Judaism and Islam. The leaders of Islam have used the United Nations, the European Union, and the United States to help them in this scheme to defeat their Zionist enemy.

However, the Islamic scheme hasn't worked because the one true God, the Lord Almighty, has had other plans, documented in Holy Scripture thousands of years ago. Those who continue to participate in this diabolical plan of Islam will eventually pay a heavy price. The Lord is using these unfolding events in the Middle East to bring our times (the church age) to a close, just as has been prophesied in the Bible.

The Muslims call this ongoing conflict a religious war, while the Jews—for the most part—do not. The Muslims want to destroy Israel, while the Jews keep indicating that they are willing to live side-by-side with their Arab neighbors.

The Muslim radicals hardly trust each other, and they can't even coexist together; and they have a long history of fighting each other. However, these sons of Ishmael apparently can come together in solidarity when the central target is Israel.

To further complicate matters, American and European business, political, and intelligence leaders continue to concern themselves with the steady flow of oil from the Middle East and its economic importance, putting these matters ahead of Israel's sovereignty.

Along with those concerns, there continue to be some strong anti-Semitic feelings. These same leaders have, for many years, especially the last twenty-plus years, had a huge impact on political matters in the Middle East and in bringing Israel to its current position of vulnerability. Unfortunately, the Israeli leaders have played directly into this charade.

The U.S. State Department and intelligence agencies have a pro-Arab history and have had a huge impact on Middle East policy. We have only had one secretary of state (before Colin Powell) in the last twenty years who was pro-Israel (Alexander Haig), and he was forced out of office because of his stance.

Even the American presidential administrations have been more pro-Arab because of the oil and the political ramifications of maintaining its steady flow to Western pipelines. There has also been no national energy policy, resulting in many questionable dealings with the world's resources by both U.S. and British oil companies and by OPEC.

Leading with this priority, these two nations have compromised Israel and her existence, both defensively and economically, for many years in an effort to appease the oil-producing Middle East nations. The U.S. has given billions in aide to Israel, but at the same time, she has armed and aided Muslim nations such as Jordan, Saudi Arabia, and Egypt. The U.S. is reported to be spending $40 billion a year through direct aide and military personnel to these nations as insurance for the flow of oil out of the Middle East.

In return, the Muslim nations have used their oil leverage in an attempt to weaken and eventually eliminate Israel. However, in reality, Israel is very capable of taking care of herself. When Israel gets to a point that she is at risk, the Bible says the Lord will powerfully intervene. As has been said before, the Muslim oil-producing nations have the world on their side, and Israel has the Lord on her side. The bottom line is that the Muslims want Israel's covenant land and want to destroy the Jews in the process. The Lord isn't happy about that, and He has responded in a timely manner. Through "acts of God" that have been tracked since October 1991, the Lord has shown that He does not want the covenant land in Israel traded for so-called "peace and security." (Refer to chapter six, "America: Blessed or Cursed?" for documentation of this response.)

Players on the Middle East Stage

The Lord has been using a variety of key players in the fulfillment of Bible prophecy pertaining to the Middle East. It is obvious who has had the clout, and it is fascinating and remarkable to review and assess how they have been and are being used. These are the people—Americans, Europeans, Israelis, and Muslims—who have shoved Israel to the brink of war. However, their actions are prime examples in today's world that they are not aware with whom they are dealing, apparently. They will soon find out, and our Lord will respond accordingly.

Former U.S. President George H. W. Bush

The current United States president's father began the Madrid conference in late 1991 with a plan for Israel to give up her covenant land in exchange for "peace and security." Bush was also responsible for bringing Arab allies together for a successful war against Saddam Hussein. However, he allowed General Colin Powell to aggressively persuade him to stop General Norman Schwartzkopf from advancing into Baghdad to capture Saddam. President

Bush continues to stay in contact with his Arab friends who are lobbying him to influence his son's activity regarding the current situation in Israel. President Bush (the elder) put together an impressive ally base for Desert Storm. Those relations deteriorated during the eight years of Clinton's tenure and the Muslims have now been unified over Israel.

Former President Bill Clinton
Clinton continued the "peace process," and on September 13, 1993, the Oslo I accords were signed at the White House in front of three thousand witnesses. The next seven years brought many more talks and new agreements with not much to show for it. In addition, America's ally, Israel, was brought to the brink of war because of faulty policy by a president who pushed Israel so he could "earn" a legacy, perhaps a Nobel prize, and—in his own words—atonement for the Monica Lewinsky matter.

Former Israeli prime ministers:
Rabin, Peres, Netanyahu, and Barak
Yitzak Rabin lost his life over what he was about to give away; Shimon Peres lost to Benjamin Netanyahu in a close election because of what he wanted to give away; Netanyahu promised a tougher line; Ehud Barak then beat Netanyahu because he was too tough and due to the fact that he allowed some of the covenant land to be given. Barak offered Syria and the Palestinians almost everything they wanted (but fortunately did not accept). The Council on Foreign Relations (CFR) was a heavy influence on each of these Israeli leaders.

Israeli Prime Minister Ariel Sharon
After the Palestinian and the Syrian refusal of Barak's astoundingly generous offer, the climate continued to worsen

politically for Ehud Barak. Ariel Sharon visited the Temple Mount on Rosh Hashanah (the Feast of Trumpets), September 28, 2000, which helped catapult him from fifteen percent in the polls to a landslide victory over Barak four months later on February 7, 2001. The now-historic Temple Mount visit gave the Palestinians and radical Muslims the excuse to begin the ongoing *intifada*.

Yasser Arafat

In 1956, Yasser Arafat founded al-Fatah, an underground terrorist organization. At first, al-Fatah was ignored by larger Arab nations such as Egypt, Syria, and Jordan, which had formed their own group—the Palestine Liberation Organization (PLO). It wasn't until the 1967 Arab–Israeli War, when the Arabs lost the Gaza Strip, Golan Heights, and West Bank, that Arab nations turned to Arafat.

In 1968, Arafat became the leader of the PLO, which launched bloody attacks on Israel, and he gained a reputation as a ruthless terrorist. But by 1988, when he told the U.N. that the PLO would recognize Israel as a sovereign state, Arafat had warmed to diplomacy. Then in 1993, Arafat met with his avowed enemies in the secret peace talks that led to the Oslo peace accords with Israeli prime minister Yitzak Rabin. The agreement granted limited Palestinian self-rule and earned Arafat, Rabin, and Israeli foreign minister Shimon Peres the 1994 Nobel Peace Prize. In January of 1996, Arafat was elected the first president of the Palestinian Council governing the West Bank and Gaza Strip.

Additionally, the Arafat regime has studied and applied the work of Dr. Joseph Goebbels, Adolph Hitler's propaganda mastermind in Nazi Germany. Goebbels hated Jews. His method was to stir something up, blame it on the Jews, and then call for martial law. Arafat follows a similar *modus operandi*; he started the violent *intifada*, blamed it on the

Jews, and then called for United Nations peacekeepers. The whole world, except the United States, now seems to be in favor of U.N. peacekeepers.

Saddam Hussein

The Iraqi dictator, reportedly on the verge of a mental breakdown at the end of the Gulf War, has been rejuvenated, and Saddam now has much of his military back, along with weapons of mass destruction (WMDs). He remains the biggest threat to Israel and to other nations in the Middle East. The United States has been focused on knocking out Iraqi radar and is rumored to be planning a much larger attack on Iraq in the very near future. Saddam called for the Iraqi formation of a seven million-person "Jerusalem Army" for the liberation of Palestine in April of 2001.

Bashar Assad

Syria's president Bashar Assad replaced his father Hafez el-Assad after his death in June 2000. He stirred things up in May by saying that Israelis are more racist than Nazis, and said, "The suffering of the Arabs under Israeli occupation is similar to the biblical suffering of Jesus Christ at the hands of first-century Jews." The tall, lanky ophthalmologist by education has surprised and shocked many with his harsh rhetoric. He has had public arguments with moderate Arab leaders. He continues to be more in line with Saddam Hussein and Yasser Arafat than Egypt's Hosni Mubarek and Jordan's King Abdullah II. Syria has relaxed the visa requirements for Iraqis coming into their country. Syria and Iraq are also the likely catalysts for increasing trouble with Israel, resulting in the possibility of that scenario becoming a regional war.

King Abdullah II

King Abdullah II commanded the elite Special Forces in

the Jordanian army and is a qualified pilot who has flown jet fighters and Cobra attack helicopters. While some may question his politics and diplomatic skills, observers say Abdullah's military background will help ensure stability in this pro-Western kingdom. Army comrades say Abdullah has shown little ambition outside the military, though he reportedly has built close links with young members of ruling Persian Gulf Arab dynasties. His government is under enormous threat from the large Palestinian population in Jordan (estimated to be fifty percent), and it has been rumored that Saddam Hussein has a plan to overthrow the king. Israel and the U.S. have both been prompt at sending in high-level military people to meet with Abdullah. General Tommy Franks, head of the U.S. Central Command, met with the king in mid-August of 2001 to discuss ways of bolstering military cooperation between the two countries.

Hosni Mubarak

Egyptian president Hosni Mubarak has been a pivotal player in the regional peacekeeping efforts. He is particularly proud of his role in the secret 1993 Norwegian talks between Israel and the PLO. He is a moderate like King Abdullah II of Jordan and together, they proposed the Egyptian–Jordanian peace initiative in late March 2001. The plan was discussed with President George W. Bush in April at the White House and was very similar to the Mitchell Plan, which is now backed by him. Mubarak and Abdullah II are the most outspoken moderates in the Mideast, while Saddam Hussein, Bashar al-Assad, and Yasser Arafat are the hard-liners.

President George W. Bush

President George W. Bush (the younger) inherited the

Mitchell Plan. U.S. Senator George Mitchell headed up a delegation that included former U.S. senator Warren Rudman and representatives of the European Union who came up with a plan for resolving the Mideast crisis. Now, with the public declaration of the "war against terrorism," President Bush is more involved than ever in the events of the Middle East.

Secretary of State Colin Powell

Secretary of State Colin Powell continues to be the moderate in the Middle East, while Vice-President Dick Cheney, Secretary of Defense Donald Rumsfeld, and National Security Advisor Condoleeza Rice continue to take the hard line. Powell has been outspoken against the targeted assassinations in which Israel is participating and has also continued to make statements that are contrary to Israel's position on key issues. His Louisville speech, on November 19, reportedly was toned down by President Bush and became a statement of the administration's Middle East position.

Vice-President Dick Cheney

Vice-President Dick Cheney was secretary of defense during Desert Storm; his team did a phenomenal job. He is practical, and he has a knack for seeing the real problems in the region for what they are. Cheney said recently he could understand Israel's "target" shootings in light of the situation they were facing. This was vintage Cheney, who tends to speak straight from the heart. Cheney was overruled during Desert Storm due to Colin Powell's lobbying of President George H. W. Bush to stop General Schwartzkopf from going into Baghdad, a decision that has come back to haunt the United States.

Prophetic Fulfillment Overtures

Men (and nations) covet oil and seek economic stability. To gain these objectives, man will rely on his own ingenuity and intellect. And yet, the Lord uses these goals and these "skills" to bring about fast-evolving events that are compatible with the prophesied end of the age. The dramatic plot of this world has now reached a very key point in human history.

Although as believers we might be disappointed and even angered by the world's super-brokers and their clandestine and covert efforts on behalf of the Middle East oil companies and producers at the risk of Israel, the Lord is using these activities to expose the world's scheme against Israel, to bring about the prophetic fulfillment of His plan according to His Word, and to evangelize more people to Him in the process.

The situation in the Middle East is at a very serious stage. Many prophecy students believe that, as the Bible forecasts in Daniel 9:27, the world is nearing the time for a "peace covenant" with many for one week (or seven-year period). However, the same verse also clarifies that this peace will only last for half that time. Concurrently, the key biblical "end-time" war scenarios appear to be approaching fulfillment. These final battles—all prophesied to take place in the Middle East—are:

- Those spoken of in Isaiah chapters thirteen, seventeen, and nineteen, having to do with the devastation of Babylon in Iraq, Damascus, Syria, and Egypt by Israel.
- Psalm 83, the regional invasion of Israel by ten former Arab nations and tribes.
- The Gog and Magog War of Ezekiel chapters thirty-eight and thirty-nine, having to do with the Russian

and Islamic invasion of Israel in which the invaders
are defeated by Israel through the Lord's supernatural help.

 • And the final battle, the Battle of Armageddon (Joel
   3:2 and Revelation 16:16), where the world's armies
   all come against Jerusalem, just prior to the second
   coming of Jesus Christ.

And lest anyone be concerned by all the war prophecy, encouragement comes from the Lord in Zechariah 12:9, where
the Lord declares: "And it shall come to pass in that day,
that I will seek to destroy all the nations that come against
Jerusalem."

Chapter 9
The Washington Connection

Therefore say, Thus saith the Lord God; I will even gather you from the people, and assemble you out of the countries where ye have been scattered, and I will give you the land of Israel.

—Ezekiel 11:17

Current United States President George W. Bush declared, in the early days of his term, that he wanted to become a facilitator, not an active participant, in the Middle East peace talks.

In an attempt to change the president's mind, Egypt's president Hosni Mubarak and Jordan's King Abdullah II both visited Washington during the first ten days of April 2001. They asked the president to become more involved in the Middle East talks and to endorse the Egyptian–Jordanian initiative, which called for Israel to freeze further settlement construction and to give up more of her land.

Additionally, the Mitchell Report (commissioned by former President Bill Clinton in October 2000) was completed on May 21. It also called for an Israeli settlement freeze and for the Palestinians to stop their terrorism. But again, the ultimate goal was for Israel to give up her covenant land in exchange for peace.

The settlements are the destination for many newcomers to Israel, those Jews who are continuing to emigrate (return) to "the Promised Land" from around the world. As has been documented in the chapter "America: Blessed or Cursed?", the Lord responds very harshly when these settlements are hindered. If returning Jews are stopped from settling in Israel, the fulfillment of God's Word is impacted. Following are three actual events that have coincided with matters having to do with Israel's "land for peace" process. These are examples of how the Lord is trying to get the attention of the Bush administration.

• March 31: On the day Egyptian president Hosni Mubarek arrived in Washington, a Chinese fighter jet "bumped" into an American EP-3 reconnaissance plane, forcing it—along with the twenty-four–person crew—to make an emergency landing in China. The resulting crisis completely overshadowed the visits of both Mubarek and King Abdullah II.

• April 10: Jordan's King Abdullah II—after arriving in Washington earlier in the week to speak with Christian leaders, members of Congress, and others to get support for the initiative—visited the White House and then returned home to Jordan. The next day, China agreed to release the "detained" airmen from the downed plane. The extremely valuable aircraft remained behind in China, evidently to be shipped home in pieces.

• May 22: President Bush and Secretary of State Colin Powell publicly endorsed the Mitchell Report. Concurrently, Vermont senator James Jeffords was rumored to be deserting the Republican Party.

• May 25: Senator Jeffords left the Republican Party, becoming an Independent, allowing the Democrats to obtain a majority in the Senate, throwing judicial and diplomatic nominations into question. On the same day, Daniel Kurtzer was nominated as ambassador to Israel, endorsed by pro-land giveaway, reform and conservative Jews who make up eighty-five percent of American Jewry.

♦ June 8: Reuters News Service reported that CIA director George Tenet and a special envoy from Washington spearheaded an international effort "to strengthen a fragile Israeli-Palestinian cease-fire" plagued by fresh violence. The CIA director hosted talks between senior Israeli and Palestinian security officials in Ramallah, while Assistant Secretary of State William Burns met Palestinian president Yasser Arafat in the West Bank. The same day, catastrophic flooding brought the Houston, Texas, area to a near standstill, with nearly ten thousand people left homeless and three thousand homes and businesses affected. Governor Rick Perry declared a state of emergency in the Houston area along with twenty-eight southeast Texas counties. More than two feet of rain fell at Bush Intercontinental Airport, causing flights to be cancelled for almost two days.

The President's Dilemma

President George W. Bush inherited the current Middle East situation from his father, George H. W. Bush, and his predecessor, Bill Clinton. The elder Bush and Clinton have been responsible for leaving the region in a very precarious position, with Israel at the brink of war. And now, the U.S. is actively involved in leading a war against terrorism, with the nations of the Middle East as key players, both as protagonists and antagonists. Presidents Bush (the elder) and Bill Clinton are both members of the Council on Foreign Relations (CFR). In fact, it was President Bush who publicly stated that success in Operation Desert Storm (the

"Gulf War") was "an example of the New World Order."

President George W. Bush has been influenced by his father's Middle East thinking. Even more significantly, he has allowed his own State Department and George Tenet, the CIA director, to influence his administration's policy toward Israel. According to a *Washington Post* article of October 2, 2001, Secretary of State Colin Powell and Tenet influenced the White House to make a public declaration in favor of a Palestinian state.

The article further stated, according to several sources familiar with the early September preparations for Powell's speech to the U.N., that the State Department, along with Tenet, had been urging other members of the administration to launch a major initiative, giving Palestinian chairman Yasser Arafat some "incentive" to halt the violence which has lasted for more than a year.

If true, this kind of thinking is an example of how uninformed our government is about the real situation in Israel. However, it is also a sign that there is likely a much larger agenda, which goes beyond Israel. No government agency in its right mind could deny the truth about Arafat's terrorist activities . . . unless they had another agenda. The State Department and the CIA know Arafat has stashed hundreds of millions of dollars in foreign bank accounts, and they know he controls the terror networks in Israel.

It is also known that the CFR has a global plan for a New World Order, and that this "council" is trying to appease the Arab states at the cost of Israel and her land. Meanwhile, Muslim nations, organizations, and influential leaders are using those CFR members in their openly-stated and diabolical attempt to destroy Israel.

The bottom line is that these world power-brokers are coming into opposition with God and the "apple of His eye," Israel. The judgment of the Lord on those who come against

Israel is well-documented in biblical history. The events of September 11, 2001, could well be the beginning of His judgment for our time.

The New Ambassador to Israel

Following is a White House press release announcing the appointment of Daniel Kurtzer to be the U.S. ambassador to Israel.

White House Press Secretary—May 25, 2001
The President intends to nominate Daniel Charles Kurtzer to be Ambassador Extraordinary and Plenipotentiary of the United States of America to the State of Israel. Ambassador Kurtzer is a career Minister in the Senior Foreign Service and has served as Ambassador to Egypt since 1997. He previously served in Washington, D.C., as Principal Deputy Assistant Secretary of State in the Bureau of Intelligence and Research from 1994 to 1997 and as Deputy Assistant Secretary in the Bureau of Near Eastern Affairs from 1989 to 1994. From 1987 to 1989, he was a Member of the Secretary of State's Policy Planning Staff and has completed several other overseas assignments. He is a graduate of Yeshiva University and received an M.A., a Ph.M. and Ph.D. from Columbia University.

The National Unity Coalition for Israel, representing two hundred Jewish and Christian organizations and 40 million Americans, opposed Kurtzer and were involved in a letter-writing campaign to President Bush.

The letter stated:

Mr. Kurtzer was a key figure in formulating the U.S. decision to recognize the PLO and Arafat as legitimate partners for "peace" with Israel. In 1988, despite the intense terrorism unleashed against Israel by the Arabs, it was Kurtzer who deceived the U.S. into believing that the PLO was a "moderate" force. He characterized PLO terrorists who massacred civilians as "guerrillas."

It was Kurtzer who promoted the recent climate of "evenhandedness" that has so distorted the truth in Middle East affairs. And it was Kurtzer who, as a speech writer for former Secretary of State James Baker, coined the term "land for peace," which led to Israel giving away its holy land for nothing but violence and lies.

For too long, Israel has suffered under the unwarranted pressure of U.S. ambassadors who have no understanding of the biblical rights of the Jewish people to the Jewish state of Israel. It is time for that pattern to be broken. Please consider our objections in evaluating Daniel Kurtzer's qualifications for the job.

We believe that, after an honest examination of his credentials, you will agree with us that Daniel Kurtzer cannot serve as U.S. Ambassador to Israel. Thank you.

However, the Central Conference of American Rabbis Rabbinical Assembly; Union of American Hebrew Congregations; and the United Synagogue of Conservative Judaism, wrote President Bush stating:

As religious movements, we rarely support or oppose Presidential appointments. Recently, however, attempts have been made by some in our community to discredit Ambassador Daniel Kurtzer from consideration as U.S. Ambassador to Israel by claiming that he holds "anti-Israel views." On behalf of the Reform and Conservative Movements, which together comprise more than eighty-five percent of affiliated American Jews, we write to indicate that such criticism is not shared by the mainstream

Jewish community. Although we would not formally support Ambassador Kurtzer's appointment, we do not believe the claim that Daniel Kurtzer is unfit to serve as Ambassador to Israel. Our movements have worked with Ambassador Daniel Kurtzer over the years and greatly respect him. He has been a committed servant of the U.S. government over the years and has been a great friend to Israel. Ambassador Kurtzer has earned broad respect in the diplomatic field among Arabs, Israelis, and American officials. We would, of course, be pleased to discuss this with you or your staff in any greater detail.

Daniel Kurtzer received his Senate confirmation and is now the U.S. ambassador to Israel.

A Presidential Response

On August 9, 2001, there was another tragic suicide bombing in Jerusalem. In response to this tragedy, President Bush issued this statement: "I deplore and strongly condemn the terrorist bombing in downtown Jerusalem today. My heartfelt sympathies and those of the American people are with the victims of this terrible tragedy and with their families."

Then he added:

The United States remains committed to implementation, in all its elements, of the Mitchell Committee Report, which provides a path to return to peace negotiations based on United Nations Security Council Resolutions 242, 338, and the Madrid Conference. To get to Mitchell, the parties need to resume effective security cooperation and work together to stop terrorism and violence.

Thus, President Bush once again called for negotiations based on U.N. Security Council resolutions and Madrid;

these agreements are in total opposition to the Lord's covenant pertaining to the land of Israel.

Palestinian State "Part of a Vision"

In a CNN report on October 2, 2001, President Bush was quoted as saying that a Palestinian state was always "part of a vision" if Israel's right to exist is respected. He said the two parties needed to "get to work on the Mitchell process," which he said provides a clear path to solving the crisis in the Middle East.

When asked, the president refused to say whether he had been prepared to announce his support for a Palestinian state prior to the September 11 terrorist attacks on Washington and New York.

The article further stated that State Department and other senior administration officials have told CNN that drafts of a major policy speech on the Middle East, to be delivered by Secretary of State Powell, were circulating within the State Department for review. These officials have said the speech will "clarify its [U.S.] views on an end result" of the Mideast peace process, which would lead to the eventual "creation of a Palestinian state."

Powell had expected to deliver the speech in late September on the sidelines of the U.N. General Assembly, but that plan was put on hold after the September 11 terrorist attacks on the World Trade Center and Pentagon. "It will go farther than we have ever gone," one official said of Powell's speech. "There is an awful lot more that we view as being the end result than what we have said so far."

One point hotly debated was whether or not to "call for ending all settlement activity," including so-called natural growth of existing settlements—something previous U.S. administrations have come close to doing, but have never done.

The same official said that such a speech would be a "powerful palliative" to the Arab world. "It eases the pain," the official said. "It would end the perception that we only move against Islam."

"We are getting hammered in the Arab world," this official said. "And it is not a mystery that one of the ways to diffuse this is to see some movement on the Israeli–Palestinian conflict."

The *Washington Post* reported that according to a source familiar with the preparation, Powell's speech was being drafted by William J. Burns, the assistant secretary of state for Near Eastern affairs, with assistance from the U.S. ambassador to Israel, Daniel Kurtzer, and Ron Schlicher, the U.S. consul general in Jerusalem. According to the National Unity Coalition for Israel, which represents two hundred Jewish and Christian organizations and forty million Americans, Kurtzer was a key figure in formulating the U.S. decision to recognize both the Palestinian Liberation Organization (PLO) and Arafat as legitimate "partners for peace" with Israel.

In 1988, despite the intense terrorism unleashed against Israel by various Islamic groups, it was Kurtzer who deceived the U.S. into believing that the PLO was a "moderate" force. He characterized PLO terrorists who massacred civilians as "guerrillas." Furthermore, it was Kurtzer who promoted the recent climate of "evenhandedness" that has so distorted the truth in Middle East affairs. And it was Kurtzer who, as a speech writer for former secretary of state James Baker, coined the term "land for peace," which led to Israel giving away its covenant land in exchange for nothing but violence and lies.

In other words, the CFR—through the State Department, the secretary of state, the CIA director, George Bush (the elder), and Bill Clinton, along with former U.S. senators George Mitchell and Warren Rudman (who are responsible for the Mitchell Plan)—is having an enormous impact on current President George W. Bush's administration and plans for the future.

God's Timing Is Perfect

The World Trade Center/Pentagon attacks stopped, temporarily, the public pronouncement of President Bush's "vision" of a Palestinian state; they kept Secretary of State Powell from making his public speech; they kept Arafat from meeting with Bush; and they postponed the U.N. General Assembly because the city of New York was not able to guarantee proper security.

In late May, Palestinian president Yasser Arafat was up against the ropes, and his government was all but defeated. Then the Bush administration sent CIA director George Tenet to Israel for meetings with the Israelis and the Palestinians on June 8. Arafat's government was again on the verge of collapse in late August and early September when the State Department acknowledged that President Bush would consider meeting with him at the General Assembly meeting scheduled to begin September 23, 2001, in New York.

Putting all these events into perspective, the State Department and the CIA—in a period of three and one-half months—bailed out Yasser Arafat twice. Then within days of the September 11 terror event, President Bush expended pressure on Israel to meet with Arafat. Ariel Sharon at first refused to approve Israeli foreign minister Shimon Peres' meeting with Yasser Arafat. He stated that negotiating with Yasser Arafat was like the U.S. trying to negotiate with Osama bin Laden.

Peres and Arafat agreed to a forty-eight–hour ceasefire, and if there weren't skirmishes, they would move on to the next phase. It failed, as previous agreements had in the past, with the loss of two Israeli lives by gunfire.

Playing the Middle East Card

Secretary of State Powell finally gave his long-awaited speech on November 19 in Louisville, Kentucky. Even though the message became the first official United States position concerning (and against) God's covenant land, it was toned down during an eleventh-hour intervention by the White House "to prevent any appearance of United States concessions being made to terrorists," according to an article in the Sydney (Australia) *Morning Herald* (November 20, 2001).

Among the points made in the message were:

♦ Israel must end its "occupation" of Palestinian territories per U.N. Resolutions 242 and 338.
♦ Israel must accept a viable Palestinian state.
♦ The "entire international community" is in favor of the Mitchell Plan.
♦ Settlement construction has severely undermined the peace process.
♦ All settlement construction must stop.
♦ "Occupation" hurts the Palestinians and affects the Israelis.

Powell's message played to rave reviews almost everywhere except Israel, where, for example, the *Arutz Sheva News* (November 20, 2001) pointed out the following:

♦ While criticizing settlement activity, Powell neglected to call for the Palestinian Liberation Organization (PLO) to cease its own construction in strategic areas—also a form of "preempting the outcome."

+ His reference to negotiation over the ultimate fate of Jerusalem could have but one outcome: Israeli concessions leading to the end of Jerusalem's status as the indivisible and eternal capital of the Jewish people.

+ The speech ignored Arafat's thirty-seven–year track record of systematically violating all his international commitments.

+ In stating that "too many innocent Palestinians, including children, have been killed and wounded," the implication is that the Palestinian "freedom fighters" (*aka* suicide bombers or terrorists) are equivalent to truly innocent Israeli civilians who lost their lives.

The lasting significance of the Louisville speech may ultimately rest in the fact that all the nations of the world have now allowed their position on God's covenant land to become public, in addition to major entities such as the World Council of Churches, the Vatican, the European Union (EU), and the United Nations.

Playing the United States Middle East card virtually completes a scenario wherein the nations have come against Israel (Zechariah 12:2–3) and the probability of a treaty (covenant) ensuring peace and security "with many" (Daniel 9:27) is very feasible. It is fascinating, prophetically, to note that the EU, along with certain nations of the Arab world, are pushing for a "two-basket deal" which calls for the establishment of a Palestinian state and the collective Arab guarantee for the security of Israel.

Opposing God's Covenant Land

Terrorism continues to force Israel to the negotiating table, not by her own wishes, but through pressure from the international community and the United States. The September 11 attacks have caused the U.S. to put great pressure on Israel to go back to the negotiating table. Even though the words have been measured, those words say much.

The following entities, representing billions of people, have spoken out against Israel and God's covenant land and/or written letters to President Bush and Secretary of State Powell:

- The Vatican
- World Council of Churches
- National Council of Churches
- The United Nations
- The European Union
- The Arab League
- China

Has there been any Christian leader who has emphasized the importance of Israel's covenant land to President Bush?

There have been a few. We have furnished letters, books, and additional material to the Bush administration who responded by saying the information was appreciated and would be provided to their policy people. Unfortunately, as previously noted, there are many other significant political entities, nations, and church organizations who look at things differently. They will soon find out that they are coming against God's covenant land, and they will be chastised for what is about to fall on our nation.

America's Response

Modern Israel has her shortcomings, just like other nations of the world, but the Lord will not allow her to be sacrificed or put at risk without responding forcefully. In addition to doling out many warnings on the same day Israel

was pushed to give up its land by three different presidential administrations over the last ten years, many questions
arise, begging for answers.

For instance, should the Christian Church in America
go unpunished for its rampant replacement theology,
naiveté, apostasy, and apathy towards Israel? How many
of the following key players in the administration ever heard
of or understood the importance of "standing by Israel" or
protecting her land?

- Former president George H. W. Bush, who is an
  Episcopalian.
- Current President George W. Bush and Vice-Presi-
  dent Dick Cheney, who are both Methodists.
- Condoleeza Rice, who is the daughter and grand-
  daughter of Presbyterian pastors.
- Chief of staff Andrew Card, who is a Methodist and
  whose wife is an ordained Methodist minister.
- Counselor to the president Karen Hughes, who is a
  Presbyterian elder.
- White House press secretary Ari Fleischer, who is a
  child of reform Jewish parents.

Former president Bill Clinton, a non-practicing Baptist,
didn't see the importance of protecting Israel's land, and
he did a lot of harm to Israel for the purpose of establish-
ing his own legacy and—as he said—to atone for his im-
proprieties.

Here is the current problem. These leaders don't understand the importance of Israel in God's plan. They speak
of lasting peace frequently, something that is not prophesied in the Bible until Jesus Christ's second coming. All
these people are good and decent people, but they are not
aware of the Abrahamic covenant, which makes it clear

that God's land is not to be given away or compromised for "peace and security."

A "Top Shelf" Staff

Most people can't even begin to comprehend the responsibility that lies on the shoulders of President Bush.

Here is the president whose plans were to be "the Education President." During his early days in office, he invoked a kinder and gentler tone in Washington, and he spoke about civility and decency in our nation. Many of his presentations and public speeches pointed out the quality of the person being honored and were very patriotic. He made reference to his Christian faith frequently and was excited by the possibilities of his Faith-Based Initiative program.

President Bush has surrounded himself with quality people in his administration. Whether members of his cabinet, his top-level administrative people, the White House staff (including the press room aides), or any other key appointees, every one of these people are "top-shelf." One of the Secret Service staff said that there has been a huge difference in the quality of people both within the Bush administration and with those visiting the White House offices, in comparison to the previous administration.

Also, the media people, despite their notorious "left-leaning" political bent, have stated that they are very impressed by the helpfulness, the punctuality, and professionalism of the press staff. The White House press secretary, Ari Fleischer, is a very good man. He is forthright, effective, and very fair. One woman, who has been part of the White House press corps for thirty-some years, said Ari is the best White House press secretary she has experienced.

Karen Hughes, who is counselor to the president and who oversees the communications staff, is delightful. She contributes a great personality, has lots of energy, and is very trustworthy. Daughter of a former Army general, she is part of "the iron triangle," along with the presidential senior advisor, Karl Rove, and FEMA director Joe Allbaugh, who formerly was the president's campaign manager.

The cabinet members are also high quality people. They might not always agree with each other or even the president on certain issues and policies, but they are very well-qualified and solid people. Sally Quinn of the *Washington Post* stated, in late January of 2001, right after the cabinet appointments were announced, that President Bush had very likely assembled the most qualified cabinet going back at least one hundred years.

Vice-President Dick Cheney is a straight-shooter with remarkable political skills. He is a good man with a lot of substance and depth. He is very likely the most influential vice-president in modern history. He demonstrates a grasp on where everything stands at all times.

Secretary of Defense Donald Rumsfeld was the youngest secretary of defense in U.S. history and has now become the oldest. He has also been the CEO of two Fortune 500 companies, was an Army wrestling champion, and is known to be tough and forthright. The nation is fortunate to have a person of his caliber at this crucial time in history.

National Security Advisor Condoleeza Rice is very capable, personable, bright, and unflappable.

Attorney General John Ashcroft is a very honorable man, who has been very outspoken about his Christian faith, and he has an extremely challenging job right now.

Secretary of State Colin Powell is a good man who wants to do well. However, he continues to check in on the wrong side of some very important issues concerning the Middle East. He is the moderate, while Cheney, Rumsfeld, and Rice are the hawks. Even so, Powell continues to have a lot of influence—along with his State Department staff—on Middle East matters.

It has become obvious that the Lord has had other plans for President Bush and his qualified staff. Regardless of any disappointment over his position pertaining to Israel's covenant land, it must be remembered that he inherited what his two predecessors (his father George H. W. Bush and Bill Clinton) left behind for him with regard to the Israeli–Palestine crisis.

We can (and should) be praying that the president and those around him will be constantly educating themselves and reevaluating their thinking and plans which involve Israel. However, that process becomes complicated by all the special interest groups, church organizations, and other nations—traditionally allies of this country—who have a different (or perhaps even no) perspective with regard to the future of God's covenant land in Israel.

Standing by Israel

Many Jews and Christians believe that President Bush is standing by Israel, and he certainly has done that in comparison to his predecessor. For example, in an August 31, 2001, *Jerusalem Post* article entitled "Carry on, President Bush" by Ron Dermer, the following was stated:

> During his election campaign, George W. Bush had this to say in a debate with Vice-President Al Gore: "I want everyone to know, should I be the president, Israel's going to be our friend. I'm going to stand by Israel."
>
> Whereas Clinton made Palestinian Authority chairman Yasser Arafat the most frequent foreign visitor to the White House, Bush has slammed the door on Arafat. Instead, he has wisely opted for disengagement, sending a message to Arafat that Uncle Sam has no intention of

rewarding him for his terrorist campaign. This message effectively removed the deadly arrow of international intervention from the Palestinian Liberation Organization leader's diplomatic quiver.

True, the State Department continues to erroneously believe that stability in the region demands placating Arab tyranny. Yet getting this institution to finally understand that the biggest threat to regional stability and American interests is the very same tyranny they are now defending will not happen overnight.

In the meantime, the President's recent remarks suggest that his years away from Washington have made him largely immune to the virus that plagues the State Department. President Bush threatened not to send an American representative to the United Nations Global Conference on Racism if the forum would be used "to pick on Israel" and "to isolate our friend and strong ally."

The Hamas-sponsored terrorist events of Saturday and Sunday, December 1 and 2, 2001, in Jerusalem and Haifa may have tipped the scale strongly in favor of supporting Israel. With twenty-five innocent Israelis dead and over two hundred thirty injured, President Bush proclaimed to the world, "I was horrified and saddened to learn of the bombings. . . . I strongly condemn them as acts of murder that no person of conscience can tolerate and no cause can justify." For the first time since the *intifada* began, no pleas to the Israeli government for restraint were forthcoming from the Bush administration.

The president charged Arafat and the Palestinian Authority to "immediately find and arrest those responsible for these hideous murders. They must also act swiftly and decisively against the organizations that support them." As of this writing, Chairman Arafat was claiming to have arrested Hamas leaders and, in English, denouncing the acts of terror. However, he reportedly was praising the suicide bombers as "martyrs" in Arabic language radio broadcasts.

God's Covenant Land

It is important to remember that the current Israeli–Palestinian scenario, the reaction of the other Arab states and the rest of the world, and the involvement of the United States is not about man's plan. It all has to do with the Lord's Abrahamic covenant, which clearly states that no land is to be given for peace.

Neither Israel nor any other nation has the power to decide the fate of God's covenant land, and the world has already seen (although without knowing) the enormous price that results when governments, organizations, or individuals attempt to use Israel's covenant land as a bargaining chip.

The world is about to collide with the Lord, who—as has been pointed out—is using Israel as the anvil. And, yes, the Bible has prophesied that world events at the end of the age would be focused on the Middle East, and specifically on Jerusalem. The headlines in the newspapers around the world have already stated that the "battle for Jerusalem" began on September 28, 2000.

The Lord's fury is building against those who would defy His Word and His commandments, especially where Israel is concerned. The Lord is bound to respond even more forcefully and succinctly, if President Bush does not respond courageously and quickly with an appropriate Bible-based decision on Israel's future. There are enormous implications for the United States based on the imminent decisions the president makes.

We need to continue to pray that President Bush makes a courageous stand to fully protect the "apple of God's eye" and God's covenant land. If he doesn't, we have been shown that there will be harsh repercussions for our nation, which will have enormous implications worldwide.

Behold, I will make Jerusalem a cup of trembling unto all the people round about, when they shall be in the siege both against Judah and against Jerusalem. And it shall come to pass in that day, that I will seek to destroy all the nations that come against Jerusalem.

—Zechariah 12:2, 9

Chapter 10
The Role of the CFR

Be not deceived; God is not mocked: for whatsoever a
man soweth, that shall he also reap. For he that soweth
to his flesh shall of the flesh reap corruption; but he that
soweth to the Spirit shall of the Spirit reap life everlasting.

—Galatians 6:7–8

Truth Does Not Go Away

Author Dr. Gary Frazier, a leading authority on Israel,
is director of Discovery Ministries in Arlington, Texas.
In his well-researched article, "The Arab/Israeli Puzzle—
Historical Facts vs. Fallacy," he says this about the current
situation in Israel:

> The fact is that Israel is reaping today the consequences
> of very bad decisions made by men in leadership who
> apparently have chosen to ignore historical truth. The
> amazing thing about truth is that it simply does not go
> away. Instead, it continues to expose lies and evil and—
> in the end—extract the full price of dishonesty, compro-
> mise, pride, and naiveté.

What Is the Council on Foreign Relations?

In Joan Veon's book *The United Nations' Global Straight-
jacket,* the author writes about the powerful and influential
members of the Council on Foreign Relations (CFR) within

the United States. The powerful men behind the 1921 CFR formation were J. P. Morgan, John D. Rockefeller, Paul Warburg, and Jacob Schiff—the very men who had engineered the Federal Reserve System in 1913.

The Council on Foreign Relations has over 3,000 members, and as of 1993, more than 670 of its members served in key positions in America: executive branch, 25; judicial branch, 5; legislative branch, 26; State Department, 63; Defense Department, 29; other cabinet departments, 12; independent agencies and corporations, 22; foundations, 83; media members, 229; corporate members, 185.

Additionally, three prominent people in the Middle East peace talks—former Secretary of State Warren Christopher, former Secretary of State Madeleine Albright, and current Secretary of State Colin Powell—are all CFR members. Also, former Secretary of Defense William Cohen, present CIA director George Tenet, Vice-President Dick Cheney, and National Security Advisor Condoleeza Rice are all CFR members.

The membership in this semi-secret group is extremely important—if not a mandatory credential—if one has aspirations of success in national politics, just as its progenitor, Masonry, was in the preceding centuries. The CFR has developed and maintained a vice-grip influence over presidential appointments. In 1988, researcher James Perloff wrote in his book *The Shadows of Power* that, since the founding of the CFR in 1921, no less than fourteen U.S. secretaries of state, fourteen treasury secretaries, and eleven defense secretaries have been CFR members. That includes every U.S. secretary of state since 1988 through to Colin Powell.

What Does the CFR Do?

The CFR has been the "initiator" and the "behind the scenes" influencer in the Middle East peace talks. It established the Middle East Forum in September of 1985, directed by Judith Kipper. The CFR internet website says that the Middle East Forum, a regional program established in Washington, D.C., in 1985,

> . . . engages key policy and opinion makers from many countries to probe vital Middle East political, economic, and strategic issues. The Forum encourages analysis of regional developments and historical perspectives in discussions of U.S. policy, as well as current political, economic, and strategic realities that affect foreign policy decision-making. The Forum focuses on American interests in the Middle East in its candid examination of regional developments with key players and a wide spectrum of area specialists and practitioners.

Reading between the lines, oil produces large amounts of income, which produces large amounts of money for United States defense contractors, building contractors, engineering firms, and oil companies with political influence. Conversely, Arab oil producers want at least a portion of Israel's land and a section of Jerusalem. They tell their "friends" at the CFR what they want, and the CFR then influences U.S. policy at the State Department and the White House in favor of their Arab friends.

The CFR has outlined its function on purpose for all to see. They are straightforward and clear in their goals. The following two paragraphs are taken from their website (*www.cfr.org/p/*):

> Founded in 1921, the Council on Foreign Relations is a nonpartisan membership organization, research center, and publisher. It is dedicated to increasing America's un-

derstanding of the world and contributing ideas to U.S. foreign policy. The Council accomplishes this mainly by promoting constructive discussions both in private and in public, and by publishing *Foreign Affairs*, the leading journal on global issues. The Council is host to the widest possible range of views, but an advocate of none, though its research fellows and independent task forces do take policy stands.

Like the great universities, foundations, and other think tanks in America, the Council on Foreign Relations aims to enhance the quality of study and debate on world issues, develop new generations of thinkers and leaders, and help meet international challenges by generating concrete and workable ideas.

More Than Just a Club

The Council on Foreign Relations holds meetings where government officials or people from foreign governments give speeches. Then a discussion follows. One former member of the CFR, economist John Kenneth Galbraith, asked, "Why should businessmen be briefed by government on information not available to the general public, especially since it can be financially advantageous?"

Five times each year, the council publishes its official journal, *Foreign Affairs*. *Time* magazine called this publication, in which future policy is discussed, "the most influential periodical in print." In addition, the CFR has a "Corporate Program" by which they indoctrinate businessmen about international matters. CFR affiliates, called "Committees on Foreign Relations," are located in thirty-eight cities in the U.S.

The Fall 1999 issue of *Foreign Affairs* is exclusively dedicated to globalization. If the past is a prelude to the future, you can expect to see more consolidations of financial conglomerates and the merging of foreign government and business activities. The CFR has exercised a decisive impact upon U.S. policy, especially foreign policy, for several decades. Primarily, it supplies personnel for upper echelon jobs. Few Americans know how the president chooses his administrators, and the majority probably trust that the most qualified were sought and found. This is not the case. It's no wonder that American policy remains the same no matter which political party is in office.

Siegman's Misguided Thinking

The most active and influential CFR member involved in the Middle East peace process has been Henry Siegman. He has written and spoken many times about his concept of Middle East peace. Look at Siegman's resumé:

Senior Fellow and Director, U.S./Middle East Project
Expertise: Middle East peace process; Arab-Israeli relations; U.S. Middle East policy; interreligious relations.

Experience: Executive Director, the American Jewish Congress (1978-94); Resident Scholar, the Rockefeller Study Center, Bellagio, Italy (1992); Founder, the International Jewish Committee for Interreligious Consultations (1968); Director, the American Association for Middle East Studies and Editor of its quarterly publication, *Middle East Studies* (1958-63):

Selected publications: *Strengthening Palestinian Public Institutions* (1999), *U.S. Middle East Policy and the Peace Process* (1997) (CFR-sponsored Independent Task Force Reports); "Arab Unity and Disunity," in *The Contemporary Middle East* (1965); author of over one hundred articles and essays on the Middle East in the *New*

York Times, Washington Post, Commentary magazine, *International Herald Tribune, The Nation, The Middle East Journal, Islamic World, Journal of Ecumenical Studies, Jerusalem Post, Al-Ahram, Al-Hayat,* and *Ashraq al-Awsat.*

Following are excerpts from two op-ed articles written for the *International Herald Tribune* by Henry Siegman. They will give you a specific example of his thinking which has influenced and positioned Israel to the brink of war.

The Truth About Jewish and Muslim
Claims to Jerusalem

by Henry Siegman—Thursday, August 10, 2000

NEW YORK—When the sages of the Talmud had irreconcilable differences over a point of theology or law, they decided to defer a decision to the Messiah, when he comes. It is a legal fiction referred to in the Talmud as *teiku. Teiku* is the only solution to the issue of sovereignty over Jerusalem's holiest site.

By every account, Israel and the Palestinians made significant progress on most of the permanent-status issues during their 15-day negotiations at Camp David. Only the issue of Jerusalem defied agreement, thus rendering all other agreements null and void. The ground rules included a clear understanding that "nothing is agreed to until everything is agreed to."

So both sides preferred to abandon historic agreements on most of the issues that divide them for the sake of retaining certain claims to sovereignty over parts of East Jerusalem.

For Israelis, a redivision of Jerusalem, which has served as the "undivided, eternal capital" of the Jewish state since 1967, is inconceivable. Equally inconceivable to Palestinians is Jewish sovereignty over Arab neigh-

borhoods in East Jerusalem, and above all over the
Haram al Sharif, on which stand the Al Aqsa and Dome
of the Rock mosques.

The surpassing irony is that by failing to reach an
accord, each side is in fact bringing about the very situation it is seeking to prevent. Israel is all but assuring
the division of Jerusalem, and the Palestinians are assuring that they will have far less access to their holiest
shrines than they now do.

(NOTE: Mr. Siegman adapted this personal comment for
the *International Herald Tribune* from an essay in the Lon-
don-based Arab monthly *Ad Diplomasi.*)

Middle East Conflict:
Seek Palestinian Confidence in What?

by Henry Siegman—Tuesday, July 17, 2001

NEW YORK—The Oslo accords failed to produce a permanent status agreement for many reasons, but primarily and most importantly because Israel never committed itself to the only goal that could have made possible
such an agreement—a viable, sovereign Palestinian state
in the West Bank and Gaza. Without such a clearly de-
fined goal, so-called confidence-building measures have
no chance whatever of achieving their purpose.

Confidence is not an abstraction that exists for its
own sake; it assumes meaning in relation to a goal—it is
confidence that the goal can be achieved. In the context
of Oslo, "confidence-building measures" can only mean
steps that lead Palestinians to believe that they will
achieve viable statehood. But if the goal of viable Palestinian statehood remains unconfirmed by Israel, as it was
under Yitzhak Rabin and Ehud Barak, or is explicitly
denied, as it has been by Ariel Sharon, what meaning

could "confidence-building measures" conceivably have? In these circumstances, incremental steps, far from building confidence, undermine it, for Palestinians fear that their adversary at the last may intend each partial measure.

The CFR and the Middle East

The CFR initiated the Mideast peace process through President George H. W. Bush in Madrid on October 31, 1991. It was continued by President Bill Clinton, and has now been inherited by current President George W. Bush. Both Bush (the elder) and Clinton are members of the CFR.

After ten years, Madrid, Oslo, Wye, and Camp David agreements have failed, and we are at the brink of war in Israel. Henry Siegman's comments are prime examples of a Jewish man who neither knows nor acknowledges the importance of God's covenant land and the importance of the Temple Mount to the Jewish people. Siegman's comments have been published throughout the world and in many Arab newspapers. He is also the key person from the CFR influencing the leaders of the Middle East and the occupants of the White House. His outrageous comments have given the Arabs fuel for their fire.

We are also hearing daily about the Mitchell Plan, conceived by former senator George Mitchell with the help of former senator Warren Rudman (both of whom are CFR members), along with three members of the European Union. Their plan calls for the cessation of terror and the freezing of settlements in Israel, designed to get the parties back to the negotiating table.

If man and his plans attempt to stop the fulfillment of God's Word in the movement of God's people back to the land of Israel by the freezing of settlement construction, a heavy price will be paid. "Therefore say, Thus saith the Lord

GOD; I will even gather you from the people, and assemble you out of the countries where ye have been scattered, and I will give you the land of Israel" (Ezekiel 11:17). Some people think the CFR is a clandestine and covert operation. Whatever the case may be, the CFR is a misguided entity seeking peace through a new world order. CFR membership includes many of the most powerful business and political leaders in the world. The problem is that the CFR relies upon its own worldly intelligence and concepts of peace and security and not the Lord's plan.

Additionally, in the CFR's Mideast planning, the organization had not figured that Syrian president Hafez el-Assad and Palestinian chairman Yasser Arafat would turn down the generous proposals, which included ninety-five percent of what they wanted, from then Israeli prime minister Ehud Barak. Now the CFR has a new hope, which is the Mitchell Plan. This too will be a major failure, and it could very likely lead to war in Israel and the Middle East.

The Council on Foreign Relations has members and policy makers at the State Department, in the White House, and at the United Nations. The current administration's national security advisor, Condoleeza Rice, whose dad and grandfather were both Presbyterian pastors, is also a CFR member. She and Secretary of State Colin Powell (also a CFR member) are the top two Bush officials who sat in on the meeting between President Bush and Israeli prime minister Ariel Sharon on June 26, 2001.

The CFR's plan has been to bring about world peace and to insure the steady flow of oil for the world's economy. Thus the CFR plan has influenced the current Middle East scenario, which is at a cataclysmic point. The CFR has also totally misunderstood (or been in total denial about) the desires of the radical Muslims, who continue to call for the destruction of Israel and her people. These Muslims do not want peace; they simply want to eliminate Israel. Henry Siegman and his CFR associates have leaned on Israel to give up her covenant land from the very beginning of the peace process.

The bottom line is that Israel should never have participated in this "land for peace" process. However, the CFR, the U.N., the White House, the State Department, and the European Union have forced them into it. Moreover, Israel's prime ministers reluctantly went along with this process, plans that were doomed for failure even before they began.

Virtually every time the "peace dream" appeared close to becoming reality, the Lord allowed circumstances to happen that stopped more of His land from being given to the Palestinians or Syrians. To document this fact, one needs only to review events such as:

♦ President George H. W. Bush's one-term administration.
♦ Israeli prime minister Yitzak Rabin's assassination.
♦ Prime Minister Netanyahu's government being voted out in a no-confidence vote.
♦ President Bill Clinton's personal problems.
♦ The death of Hafez el-Assad, president of Syria.
♦ Prime Minister Barak's government being voted out in a no-confidence vote and then losing to Ariel Sharon by a landslide. This major political change in Israel happened after Barak's enormous land offerings to the Palestinians and Syrians.

Wishful Thinking

Jewish and Arab businessmen have been proud of their efforts in the planning behind the scenes of the Oslo accords. A prominent Jewish businessman in Dallas proudly shared pictures of his Arab and Jewish counterparts along with Yasser Arafat. This man really believed there would finally be lasting peace in Israel. Talk about wishful thinking! It has been a total failure, and worse yet: it has put Israel at great risk. It is remarkable how many people have been involved, at many levels, all over a small amount of land in Israel.

Unfortunately, the radical Muslims, who took control once the peace talks began, caught this very nice and honorable man, a conservative Jew, off guard. It was not the diplomats in charge; it has been the terrorists. In addition, this man was not aware that the land they were trading for peace was the land that God gave to Israel. He did not understand that this land was not to be given away for peace and security. He certainly wasn't aware of the importance of the Abrahamic covenant.

However, all of this hasn't surprised those who are prophetically tuned into the significance of what has happened in Israel in the last ten years. As much as anyone has cringed to see what has transpired, along with the U.S. role, there shouldn't be any surprises because this has all been prophesied in our Bible.

Kissinger's Revelation

Former U.S. secretary of state Henry Kissinger, a CFR member, was one of the main "behind-the-scenes" architects of the Middle East peace plan. He has also had a lot of influence over many Israeli prime ministers. The answer he gave in a Cable News Network (CNN) chat room question (below) was very revealing. He acknowledged that a practical arrangement for coexistence is the priority rather than a comprehensive plan like the one discussed at Camp David in July 2000. He is acknowledging that the sweeping efforts didn't work.

CNN chatroom participant: Have U.S. efforts to resolve the Middle East conflict been effective to date? Should the U.S. do more to ensure calm in the region?

Kissinger: The United States has played a major role, but it sometimes has made mistakes by not understanding the nature of the conflict. For example, last year, President Clinton attempted—with very high motives—to bring about a permanent settlement. But a permanent settlement in the Middle East involves so many religious and deep-seated emotions, that the most extreme elements had a focal point around which to rally. So, the interest was the present intense conflict in the region. Therefore, when we go back to negotiations, we should strive for practical arrangements of coexistence, rather than sweeping attempts like last year.

In reality, the offerings of the Camp David meetings will never be available again. The Palestinians rejected prime minister Ehud Barak's astounding and generous offer, and they still aren't satisfied. The Israelis will never again offer anywhere near what they did at Camp David, and hardliner Ariel Sharon is now the prime minister. This scenario could easily create the perfect ingredients for war.

Enter Colin Powell

The U.S. Secretary of State, yet another CFR member, played America's Middle East card in his speech at Louisville on November 19, 2001. Whether his proposals—reportedly toned down by the White House—carried the mission statement of the CFR or not, they definitely were in favor of a Palestinian state, the "land for peace" principle, and a halt to settlement activity.

Frank J. Gaffney, president of the Center for Security Policy and a columnist for the *Washington Times*, wrote on November 11, 2001, that Colin Powell's tenure at the State Department has become a "case of what might be considered chronic insubordination" in his relationship with President Bush.

In solving the Palestinian-Israeli conflict, he wrote:

> Mr. Powell is working hard to arrange a . . . pass for Yasser Arafat. If Mr. Powell succeeds in transforming the proto-state Palestinian Authority—which harbors, trains, arms, feeds, and funds terrorists every day—into an actual terrorist-sponsoring state of "Palestine," President Bush will be surprised to discover that his commitment to an Israel living as a "Jewish state in peace and security" in the Middle East will be rendered meaningless.

Wherefore hear the word of the LORD, ye scornful men, that rule this people which is in Jerusalem. Because ye have said, We have made a covenant with death, and with hell are we at agreement; when the overflowing scourge shall pass through, it shall not come unto us: for we have made lies our refuge, and under falsehood have we hid ourselves.

—Isaiah 28:14–15

Chapter 11
The World Comes Against Israel

The burden of the word of the LORD for Israel, saith the
LORD, which stretcheth forth the heavens, and layeth the
foundation of the earth, and formeth the spirit of man
within him. Behold, I will make Jerusalem a cup of trembling unto all the people round about, when they shall
be in the siege both against Judah and against Jerusalem.

—Zechariah 12:1–2

A lot has changed in the Middle East over the past ten
years since the peace process began. The current status reflects a result of governments and leaders not understanding and knowing the importance of God's covenant
land in Israel. One need only look at what has happened to
those responsible for partitioning, trading, or tampering
with this land; they have been taken out of the way by death,
or they have lost their political office. Meanwhile, the situation in Israel and the Middle East has continued to dete-
riorate. To this day, there is but a small group of people in
the world who are aware of the consequences for coming
against God's covenant land.

Quite simply, all Israel wanted in the first place was to
be left alone. Defensively, it was crucial for her to keep the
land—her covenant land—obtained in the 1967 war. However, the Muslims also wanted this land, and they have used
terrorism, propaganda, and the influence of their vast oil

reserves to bring Israel to the negotiating table. The Arab nations, descendants of Abraham through Ishmael, have been a thorn in Israel's side for thousands of years.

> And the Angel of the Lord said unto her [Sarah], Behold, thou art with child, and shalt bear a son, and shalt call his name, Ishmael; because the Lord hath heard thy affliction. And he will be a wild man; his hand will be against every man, and every man's hand against him; and he shall dwell in the presence of all his brethren.
>
> —Genesis 16:11–12

The Historical Perspective

The following information came from the government of Israel and from the ultimate source, the Bible, God's inspired, infallible, and inerrant Word. Israel became a people and a nation more than thirty-two hundred years ago, some two thousand years before the advent of Islam. By contrast, Palestinian nationalism first began to flicker sometime in the late nineteenth century, just over one hundred years ago.

After Joshua conquered the country, the Jews controlled it almost without interruption for some seven hundred years. Since the destruction of the second Temple and the dispersion—about A.D. 70—until this day, there has been a continuous Jewish presence in the land.

King David made Jerusalem the capital of his kingdom, and Jerusalem was the capital of the Jewish states in Eretz Israel thereafter. In about thirteen hundred years of Muslim control, Jerusalem never once was the capital of any Muslim political entity. Jerusalem is a city holy to the Jewish people. It is mentioned more than eight hundred times in the Bible. By contrast, the Qur'an (Muslim Koran) does not mention Jerusalem even once.

The first and second Jewish Temples stood on Mount Moriah in Jerusalem. That location, known as the Temple Mount, is where Abraham, the father of the Jews, was tested by God to sacrifice his son Isaac (Genesis 22:1–19). The Muslims built their Dome of the Rock on the Temple ruins. When Jews pray, anywhere, they face towards Jerusalem. In contrast, Muslims face towards Mecca when they pray.

The number of Arab refugees who fled Palestine in the war that they instigated, is estimated at six hundred thirty thousand. Most fled without having seen a single Israeli soldier. The Arab countries deliberately refrained from absorbing the refugees, even though this was territorially, culturally, and economically feasible. Of approximately 100 million refugees in the world since the end of World War II, these Palestinians are the only group that has neither been taken in, nor have they been integrated.

At the end of World War II, there were about one million Jewish refugees in Europe. At the end of Israel's war of independence, there were hundreds of thousands of Jewish refugees from Arab countries. Israel, a country no larger than New Jersey, has absorbed them all, plus countless others from around the world. The population of Israel today surpasses six million.

Israel guarantees freedom of religion and worship for all creeds. Jews, Christians, Muslims, Druze, Samaritans, and Bahai may freely pray at their own holy places and houses of worship. This is not so in Arab countries. The Hashemite kingdom of Jordan, for example, did not honor the clauses in its 1949 armistice agreement with Israel, and did not allow Jewish worshippers access to their holy places. In the recent fighting, the Palestinians have displayed their "tolerance" by torching Joseph's tomb, near Nablus, and turning it into a mosque. They also set the ancient synagogue in Jericho ablaze, and relentlessly attacked Jewish worshippers at Rachel's tomb.

There is only one state of Israel, but many Arab countries. The Arabs have exploited their numerical edge to pass anti-Israel resolutions in the United Nations and other international organizations. This not only cheapens these institutions' resolutions, but also diverts them from their missions, which are to be dealing with the serious problems that beset the world.

The Changing Middle East Scene

The United States has lost her Arab alliance base, whose central target and concern is now on Israel and not Iraq. The Middle East has become a more dangerous place due to the acquisition of weapons of mass destruction. Russia and China are flexing some muscle in the region on the sides of those nations opposed to Israel. The United Nations continues to exert increasing pressure on Israel. The European Union, and many other entities, press for international peace monitors. The whole region is on the verge of war, which is now even more probable following the U.S. declaration of war on terrorism.

The United States has been a good friend to Israel, defending her and providing much-needed military equipment and billions of dollars in financial aide over the years. However, this relationship began to change when the peace process was initiated, and the process has put Israel in a very tenuous and precarious position, beginning with the administration of President George H. W. Bush (the elder).

In the past three years, most of Israel's Arab neighbors, openly avowed to be enemies of Zion, have obtained weapons of mass destruction. In addition, China and North Korea are now supplying arms to Libya, Iran, Iraq, and Syria, while Russia continues to supply weapons to Syria and Iraq and has recently signed agreements with Iran and Libya. China has an enormous appetite for oil and is continuing to increase her influence in the Middle East. Moreover, China seems to enjoy being an obstacle to the United States wherever and whenever possible, and she continues to intentionally not see "eye to eye" with the United States on many different matters.

Since the peace process began, Israel has reluctantly tried to please everybody and believed that there might be a chance at a lasting peace. Unfortunately, that strategy has proved to be wrong. The Arabs—especially the Muslim states—openly want to eliminate Israel. Ultimately, however, the Lord has other plans for His chosen people. Time after time, man thinks he has the solution, but God responds by proving that His ways are not the world's ways.

Current Pressures on Israel

In an August 2001 meeting, the Arab foreign ministers declared that Jerusalem is an Islamic Arab-Palestinian city, and they rejected all forms of "Judaization" of the city. They also repeated previous pledges to shower urgent assistance on the Palestinian people, both financially and morally. However, it's important to know that it isn't just the Arab-Muslim factions coming against Israel and Jerusalem. Here are other groups who have pressured and are pressuring Israel to give up her covenant land:

+ The Council on Foreign Relations (CFR) continues, even to this day, to provide political and economic pressure on Israel.
+ Many reform and conservative Jews have been hopeful that "land for peace" negotiations would be successful.
+ The administration of former U.S. president George H. W. Bush was hopeful that "land for peace" would

work. Bush hoped to appease his Arab friends and, at the same time, still keep Israel happy.

• The U.S. State Department efforts have been aligned with the Arabs for many years. In addition, every secretary of state since 1949 has been a member of the CFR.

• The Vatican and Pope John-Paul II drool over Jerusalem. They have used political, religious, and economic influences to get their hands on Jerusalem. They even signed an agreement with the Palestinians (representing 1.2 billion Muslims) on February 15, 2001, calling for Jerusalem to be shared between the three great world religions. Israel did not sign.

• The World Bank has placed economic pressure on Israel, with the intention of appeasing the Arab oil-producing nations.

• The International Monetary Fund (IMF) has also exerted economic pressure on Israel for the same reason, and is also concerned with the loan quality of Israel's debt.

• Since 1967, the U.N., spearheaded by twenty-one Arab states, has launched over a thousand one-sided anti-Israel resolutions, but has never once explicitly condemned any Arab terrorism against the citizens or the state of Israel. Of the one hundred seventy-five U.N. Security Council resolutions passed before the year 1990, ninety-seven were directed against Israel. The only countries that continue to vote consistently with Israel are the U.S. and Micronesia.

• The foreign ministers of the G-8 industrialized countries (U.S., U.K., Italy, Germany, France, Canada, Japan, and Russia), at their July 19–21, 2001, Genoa conference, in a strongly-worded communiqué on the situation in Israel, backed the call for independent observers to be deployed in Israel. The G-8 leaders' statement said: "The urgent implementation of the Mitchell Report is the only way forward. The cooling off period must begin as soon as possible. Violence and terrorism must stop. Third-party monitoring, accepted by both parties, would serve their interests in implementing the Mitchell Report." Senator Mitchell's report called for an end to violence, a crackdown on terrorists and militants by the Palestinian Authority, and a freeze on the building of Jewish settlements in the West Bank and Gaza.

♦ The European Union has had a major influence in the talks, has a closer relationship with the Arab nations, and is also in favor of peace monitors. Yuval Steinetz, a member of the Knesset (Likud Party), stated a careful analysis of the two common European positions: the support for the Palestinians' "right of return" and the objection to almost any Israeli defense operation, suggesting that Israel's adversaries in the Middle East might find some hidden partners in their mission to destroy the Jewish state. (Members of the European Union are U.K., Germany, France, Italy, Ireland, Sweden, Finland, Denmark, Portugal, Belgium, Netherlands, Austria, Luxembourg, Greece, and Spain.)

♦ Russia has a history of relationships with Arab nations. They have supplied billions of dollars of weapons to Muslim states in the Mideast. They have a very good relationship with Iraq, Iran, and Syria. In a recent Anti-Defamation League survey, forty-four percent of Russians stated they hold strong anti-Semitic views; ninety-three percent believe that Jews have too much power in the world of business; eighty-one percent believe Jews in Russia these days exercise too much power; sixty-nine percent think that Jews are more unscrupulous than others; and seventy-five percent believe that Jews are unconcerned about other ethnic groups.

♦ Chinese president Jiang Zemin vowed on August 24, 2001, to continue backing Palestinian Authority chairman Yasser Arafat's stance in Mideast peace negotiations and condemned Israel's use of "excessive force." As Arafat said afterward, he was "very satisfied" with China's support. "Our support to the just cause of the Palestinian people resuming their national rights is consistent and firm," state television quoted Jiang as telling Arafat during talks in Beijing. "The Chinese people will always stand on the side of the Palestinians' just cause and support all efforts from the international community aimed at ending the conflict," Jiang said.

♦ The final declaration of the U.N. World Conference Against Racism, adopted September 8, 2001, in Durban, South Africa, is accompanied by a program of action, including the following points on the Israeli-Palestinian situation: "We [U.N. World Conference] are concerned about the plight of the Palestinian people under foreign occupation. We recognize the inalienable right of the Palestinian people to self-determination and to the establishment of an independent state. We recognize the right to security for all states in the region, including Israel. We call upon all states to support the peace process and bring it to an early conclusion. We recognize the right of [Palestinian] refugees to return voluntarily to their homes and properties in dignity and safety, and urge all states to facilitate such return."

♦ The following nations possess biological weapons:

Iraq, Iran, Syria, Libya, China, North Korea, Russia, Israel, Taiwan, and possibly Sudan, India, Pakistan, and Kazakhstan. According to intelligence sources in Europe and the United States, terrorist groups across the globe are now developing or seeking to purchase biological weapons. Many of these nations have a large Muslim population. Many are within close proximity to or border on Israel. Also, most of these countries are archenemies of Israel and, to a certain extent, the United States.

♦ The fifty-seven–nation Organization of Islamic States Conference takes a vocal stand against Israel.

♦ The world's media flagrantly continues to side with the Muslim nations against the Jews. Their photographs dramatically portray the Palestinian injuries or deaths, but seldom those of the Jews. Their articles are constantly biased in favor of the Muslims.

Religious Organizations Against Israel

♦ In the Sunday, May 6, 2001, *Jerusalem Post*, Pope John-Paul II said he was in Syria to encourage all sides in the Arab-Israeli conflict to change their attitudes and seek lasting peace. "My pilgrimage is also an ardent prayer of hope," said the pope, who then traveled to Kuneitra in the Golan Heights where he prayed for peace. "It is time to return to the principles of international legality: the banning of acquisition of territory by force, the right of peoples to self-determination, respect for the resolutions of the United Nations, and the Geneva convention."

♦ On August 3, 2001, a World Council of Churches (*www.wcc-coe.org/wcc/english.html*) consultation on the Israeli-Palestinian problem decided, in coordinated ecumenical action, to form a small group for the purpose of developing "realistic" proposals for action with local and international partners in seven areas:

· coordinating advocacy with governments.

· boycotting goods produced in Israeli settlements in the "occupied" territories.

· strengthening the "chain of solidarity" through prayer vigils.

· resisting the destruction of property and uprooting of people from their homes and land.

· encouraging and enabling the presence of ecumenical monitoring teams.

· improving communication, interpretation, and media reporting on the conflict and its causes.

· increasing church, ecumenical, and interreligious delegations to and from Israel and the "occupied" Palestinian territory.

♦ The National Council of Churches (*www.ncccusa.org*) stated on August 30, 2001: "In previous statements and related actions, we have affirmed our support for the rights of Palestinians, for a shared Jerusalem, and for reconciliation and peace with justice in the Holy Land. . . . Moreover, we are asking the Bush administration to support the deployment of multinational observers with the aim of promoting peace, justice and security in the Occupied Territories. Our churches seek to be agents of reconciliation and of peace among people of all faiths, ethnicities, and cultures. Therefore, with you, we will continue to urge both the government of Israel and the Palestinian Authority to end the cycle of violence, which increasingly is destroying human lives and property and defiling holy places. We call upon both parties to resume dialogue toward the day when all in the Holy

Land can live in justice and peace."

♦ The text of a letter from eighteen U.S. church leaders, June 7, 2001, to U.S. Secretary of State Colin Powell (Documentation: "Eighteen Churches Back Freezing Settlements and Call Israeli Action a Violation of International Law and U.N. Resolutions"): "Few things have done more to destroy the hope and pursuit of peace through negotiations than Israel's unrelenting settlement activity. Over these recent years, we have heard from our Palestinian Christian partners, and seen for ourselves, the destructive impact of Israel's settlement policy—separating village from village, confiscating more and more Palestinian land, creating friction with its military checkpoints.

"For over twenty years our churches have appealed to the U.S. government to require Israel to cease this transfer of its civilian population into occupied territory, a clear violation of international law and United Nations resolutions. Each administration has spoken in opposition to the settlement activity, only to watch the settlements increase and expand as Israel ignores the advice. It is time for the United States to do what it must to bring Israel's settlement activity to an end.

"We urge you to make clear to Israel and the Palestinians that the United States is committed to a negotiated end of Israel's military occupation of the Gaza Strip, the West Bank, and East Jerusalem as called for in U.N.S.C. Res. 242, and that an immediate freezing by Israel of its settlement activity, including natural growth, is imperative. It will likely require considerable diplomatic pressure, and possibly economic pressure as well, to convince the government of Israel to recognize that this is a major policy concern of the United States."

Representatives from the following organizations signed this letter: National Council of Churches; the Episcopal Church; the Armenian Orthodox Church; Catholic Conference of Major Superiors of Mens' Institutes; Evangelical Lutheran Church in America; Greek Orthodox Archdiocese of America; the United Methodist Church; African Methodist Episcopal Church; American Baptist Churches USA; Antiochian Orthodox Christian Archdiocese of North America; Christian Church (Disciples of Christ) in the United States and Canada; Church of the Brethren General Board; the Evangelical Lutheran Church in America; International Council of Community Churches; Korean Presbyterian Church in America; Mennonite Central Committee; Moravian Church—Northern Province; Presbyterian Church (USA); Reformed Church in America; Syrian Orthodox Church of Antioch for the Eastern USA; Unitarian Universalist Association; United Church of Christ.

In Support of Israel

On the other side of the spectrum, the only groups who are consistently outspoken in favor of Israel keeping her covenant land include:

- Orthodox Jews.
- Small number of reform and conservative Jews.
- Israeli settlers and residents of the Golan Heights.
- Fundamental (Bible-believing) Christians.

Current Threats to Israel

Economic

The Arab League has threatened a boycott on Israeli exports; in addition, they are behind the Mitchell Plan. The European Union (EU) has also threatened a boycott on Israeli exports, and they are also behind the Mitchell Plan. Both the World Bank and the IMF have threatened further pressure on existing loans and new loans to Israel. In addition, they are behind the Mitchell Plan.

Political

Both the Bush White House and the United Nations (U.N.) have expressed their support for the Mitchell Plan.

In February of 2002, a unanimous consensus of fourteen EU ministers called for immediate establishment of a Palestinian state, election of Palestinian officials, and admittance to the U.N. as a "starting point" for any further negotiations in the peace process.

The U.N. votes are always overwhelmingly against Israel, and the organization continues to hold out permanent membership to Israel as a carrot.

In Durban, South Africa, the United States and Israel both walked out of the U.N. World Conference Against Racism on September 3, 2000, in protest of a draft of the conference's final declaration that denounced "practices of racial discrimination against the Palestinians as well as other inhabitants of the Arab occupied territories" by Israel and that said Zionism "is based on racial superiority."

Israeli foreign minister Shimon Peres, explaining the Israeli decision to withdraw from the conference, said, "We regret very much the very bizarre show in Durban. An important convention that was supposed to defend human rights became a source of hatred, a show of unfounded accusation, a reverse to every responsibility on the international arena. . . . I want also to express my thanks to forty-three countries that took a clear position against this unbelievable attempt to smear Israel with false colors."

The U.N. Security Council has been debating sending international peace monitors to watch over matters in Israel, but the U.S. veto has stopped the plan from being approved.

Terrorism

The terrorism and fighting has had a dramatic impact on Israel's economy. In the long run, this could be disastrous. During the fourth quarter of 2000, visitor entries to Israel plunged fifty-four percent compared to the same period in 1999, according to the Central Bureau of Statistics. Tourism is reported to be off eighty percent since the *intifada* began. Some hotels have closed, and many have drastically reduced their staffs. Bethlehem is now totally shut down to tourists.

The Bank of Israel reported that foreign investment dropped 58.7 percent in the first five months of 2001, to $2.2 billion as compared to $5.3 billion during the corresponding period of 2000. The unemployment rate in the country has risen to ten percent.

Who Are (or Have Been) the Players?

It is fascinating to take note of the world leaders who have been involved in the Israeli peace talks, a nation that has only 7,961 square miles (the size of New Jersey); a population of 6.4 million (5.2 million Jews); a GDP in 1997 that was $92.3 billion (U.S.), with imports $44.07 billion (U.S.) and exports $31. 5 billion (U.S.).

Israel is a very small (yet productive) nation, so why all the attention? It has to do with appeasing the Arab oil producers and the impact that oil has on their respective nation's economies, to the wishful thinking of some Jewish leaders and the pressure they have been under to participate in a "land for peace" dream, to the anti-Semitic feelings existing among many world leaders; and to the long-standing Muslim goal to eliminate Israel and its people. Listed below are the main power brokers who have been involved. This is a remarkable list of the world's most powerful leaders—Israelis, Muslims, Americans, Europeans, and U.N. participants. Yes, it is astounding that all these people have been involved in the talks over the land of a tiny Middle East nation. Unbeknownst to them, they have come (and are coming) into direct conflict with the Lord Almighty over His covenant land.

Israel's Leaders

- Prime Minister Yitzhak Rabin
- Prime Minister Shimon Peres
- Prime Minister Benjamin Netanyahu
- Prime Minister Ehud Barak
- Prime Minister Ariel Sharon

Muslim Leaders

- Palestinian Authority chairman Yasser Arafat
- Former Jordanian president King Hussein
- Current Jordanian president King Abdullah II
- Former Syrian president Hafez el-Assad
- Current Syrian president Bashar el-Assad
- Egyptian president Hosni Mubarek

Nixon and Reagan Administrations

- Former President Ronald Reagan (not CFR, not anti-Israel, or anti-Semitic, but concerned about the flow of oil)
- Secretary of State Henry Kissinger (Jewish, but compromised Israel)
- Secretary of State George Shultz (pro-Arab)

- CIA director William Casey (pro-Arab)
- Secretary of State Alexander Haig (pro-Israel)
- Secretary of Defense Caspar Weinberger (pro-Arab)

President George H. W. Bush's Administration

- Former President George H. W. Bush (not anti-Israel or anti-Semitic, but has many friends in the Arab nations due to oil interests and the Gulf War, aka Desert Storm)
- Secretary of State James Baker (pro-Arab)
- Special Assistant to the Secretary of State Richard Perle (pro-Arab)

President Bill Clinton's Administration

- Former President Bill Clinton (pro-Arab)
- Secretary of State Warren Christopher (pro-Arab)
- Secretary of State Madeleine Albright (pro-Arab)
- State Department Middle East envoy Dennis Ross (Jewish, but pro-land giveaway)

President George W. Bush's Administration

- President George W. Bush (not CFR, position still developing, but seemingly sympathetic toward Israel and obviously walking a fine line)
- Vice-President Dick Cheney (most pro-Israel member of Bush administration, his oil company had many Arab customers)
- Secretary of State Colin Powell (position still developing, diplomatic, moderate)
- National Security Advisor Condoleeza Rice (position still developing, not a Middle East student, but sides with Cheney's and Rumsfeld's tough line on the Middle East)
- Secretary of Defense Donald Rumsfeld (not CFR, favors strong action against militant Arab groups)

Jewish Businessmen

- Edgar Bronfman (president of the World Jewish Congress; owner of the *Jerusalem Report*)
- Charles Bronfman (brother of Edgar Bronfman; appointed chair of a super-Jewish organization created by melding the United Jewish Appeal, United Israel Appeal, and Council of Jewish Federations; owner of key industries in Israel)
- Conrad Black (chairman of the Hollinger Corporation, owner of the *Jerusalem Post;* a major client of Henry Kissinger Associates)
- Henry Siegman (senior fellow at the CFR; former national director of the American Jewish Congress and the Synagogue Council of America; heads the CFR's Middle East task force)
- Ronald Lauder (as of February 1999 chair of the Presidents of Major Jewish Organizations)
- David Kemche (chair of Israel's Council on Foreign Relations)

European Union

- Spain's King Juan Carlos
- French president Jacques Chirac
- British prime minister Tony Blair
- German president Helmut Kohl
- German chancellor Gerhard Schroeder
- German foreign minister Joschka Fischer
- European Union policy chief Javier Solana
- EU Middle East envoy Miquel Moratinous

United Nations Secretaries-General

- Boutros Boutros-Ghali
- Kofi Annan

Vatican

   ✦ Pope John-Paul II

Vatican-Palestinian Agreement

The audacity of Pope John-Paul II is amazing. One month before he came to Israel to formally ask forgiveness for the Vatican's role during the Holocaust, he made an agreement with Palestinian Authority chairman Yasser Arafat concerning Jerusalem. He did not consult the Israelis before this was done. What was the purpose? Why did he side with Islam? Did he forget that Islam is the religion that persecutes and imprisons Christians for sharing the gospel in their nations? He stated that he (speaking on behalf of the Roman Catholic Church, one assumes) wants to share Jerusalem with Muslims and the Jews. This was a flagrant attempt to legitimize not only Islam and its claim on Jerusalem but also the Catholic Church claim.

The Vatican-Palestinian agreement, signed on February 15, 2000, stated the following:

> An equitable solution for the issue of Jerusalem, based on international resolutions, is fundamental for a just and lasting peace in the Middle East, and that unilateral decisions and actions altering the specific character and status of Jerusalem are morally and legally unacceptable; Calling, therefore, for a special statute for Jerusalem, internationally guaranteed, which should safeguard the following:
>
> (a) Freedom of religion and conscience for all.
>
> (b) The equality before the law of the three monotheistic religions and their Institutions and followers in the City.
>
> (c) The proper identity and sacred character of the City and its universally significant, religious, and cul-

tural heritage.

(d) The Holy Places, the freedom of access to them and of worship in them.

(e) The Regime of "Status Quo" in those Holy Places where it applies.

The Israelis responded by saying:

> Israel expresses its great displeasure with the declaration made today in Rome by the Holy See and the PLO, which includes the issue of Jerusalem, and other issues which are subjects of the Israeli-Palestinian negotiations on permanent status. The agreement signed by these two parties constitutes a regretful intervention in the talks between Israel and the Palestinians.
>
> Furthermore, there is no denying that Israel safeguards freedom of conscience and freedom of worship for all, and provides free access to the holy places of all faiths. Similarly, there is no question that the religious and cultural character of Jerusalem is being preserved, as are the rights of all the religious communities and their institutions in the city. Consequently, Israel flatly rejects the reference to Jerusalem in the aforementioned document. Jerusalem was, is, and shall remain the capital of the State of Israel, and no agreement or declaration by these or any other parties will change this fact.

The pope has continued to meet with PLO chairman Arafat, who has been in the Vatican nine times since 1994.

Prophecy and the Pope

On Saturday, May 6, 2001, Pope John-Paul II called for "lasting peace" in the Middle East on his trip to Syria. If only the pope would take the time to familiarize himself with Bible prophecy, both fulfilled and unfulfilled, he would be speaking differently.

As Bible prophecy scholars and students know, lasting Middle East peace is not part of the Lord's plan. Yes, there will be a seven-year peace covenant, according to Daniel 9:27, but the peace won't last any longer than forty-two months. Additionally, one must consider the impact that the pope's comments might have on many members of the Roman Catholic Church, an organization of 900 million followers. Could the major apostasy, about which the Bible speaks in the "final days," be centered in the Catholic Church?

In the *Jerusalem Post*, the pope said he was in Syria to encourage all sides in the Arab-Israeli conflict to change their attitudes and seek lasting peace. "My pilgrimage is also an ardent prayer of hope," he said. "It is time to return to the principles of international legality: the banning of acquisition of territory by force, the right of peoples to self-determination, respect for the resolutions of the United Nations, and the Geneva convention."

Putting the pope's words into perspective, he not only called for lasting peace, but he also called for the Middle East parties to respect the United Nations resolutions. In other words, the pope has asked Israel to give up her land in exchange for peace.

Syrian Pressure on the Pope

In the May 7, 2001, *Jerusalem Post*, Syrian president Bashar el-Assad was quoted as telling Pope John-Paul II, "We feel that in your prayers, in which you recall the suffering of Jesus Christ, you will remember that there is a people in Lebanon, the Golan [Heights], and Palestine, that is suffering from subjugation and persecution." Assad then told the pope, "We expect you to stand by them [these peoples] against the oppressors [Israel] so that they can regain what was unjustly taken from them."

Assad, who stirred up a storm in March by saying that Israelis are more racist than the Nazis, said, "the suffering of the Arabs under Israeli occupation is similar to the biblical suffering of Jesus Christ at the hands of first-century Jews."

The pressure continues to mount on Israel to give up her land. And now, the pope, who is the spiritual leader of 900 million Catholics, along with the leaders of 1.2 billion Muslims, is calling for Middle East peace and blaming Israel for being in the way. Our Lord will not be happy with this, and He will respond according to the prophecies of the Bible.

Egypt said that it would join Syria in a war against Israel. This threat—in addition to the obstinate attitude of Syria, Saddam Hussein's formation of a "Jerusalem Army" in Iraq, and the terrorist antics of Palestinian Authority chairman Arafat—has many prophecy scholars saying that war, with these nations coming against Israel, appears to be imminent.

In Retrospect

From the vantage point of the current moment, Israel should have refused any participation in negotiations for the partitioning of their land in exchange for the hopes of peace and security. However, the Council on Foreign Relations (CFR), the World Bank, the European Union (EU), the Russians, the Arab League, former United States President George H. W. Bush, and former Secretary of State Jim Baker all have pressured Israel into "land for peace" talks.

In addition, the United Nations (U.N.) has been putting pressure on Israel to accept Resolutions 242 and 338, which call for Israel to "give back" the land she obtained in the 1967 war, land that is crucial to their security. (Note that Israel is not even asking for all the land spelled out in the Abrahamic Covenant.) Oil-rich Arab leaders have pressured the CFR, Bush (the elder), and Baker, who in turn began pressuring the leadership in Israel. No one would have cared or responded if the Arabs did not have the much needed and coveted petroleum raw materials.

In addition, influential members of reform and conservative Jews (comprising eighty-five percent of American Jewry) have been in favor of, and even backed, the "land for peace" concept. Moreover, they wrote current President George W. Bush a letter to affirm their support for Daniel Kurtzer as the nominee for U.S. ambassador to Israel.

The upshot is that, even though there was reluctance by Israeli government officials to participate in any "land for peace" plan, there have been many forces using their influence to motivate their decision toward that end or attempting to pressure Israel to participate.

In hindsight (but perhaps not in Bible prophecy), the whole Middle East peace process has turned out to be a major mistake. The world and its leaders have come and are coming against Israel, the "apple of God's eye," and the Lord Almighty is about to come against those nations of the world who are attempting to inflict harm upon Israel. "And it shall come to pass in that day, that I will seek to destroy all the nations that come against Jerusalem" (Zechariah 12:9).

Chapter 12

Jerusalem:
A Burdensome Stone for the Nations

And in that day will I make Jerusalem a burdensome
stone for all people: all that burden themselves with it
shall be cut in pieces, though all the people of the earth
be gathered together against it.

—Zechariah 12:3

The Bible does not end with the rebirth of the nation of
Israel, but goes into great detail about what happens
after the nation is reborn. The Bible shows the reborn nation of Israel will be rejected and suffer war after war. The
wars that Israel has gone through since its rebirth along
with the rejection of the nation by nearly all religious, political and economic organizations fits right into Bible
prophecy. The wars involving Israel in 1948, 1956, 1967
and 1973 are minor compared to the future battles described
in the Bible. These wars against God's covenant people will
not go on forever. There will be an end to the wars. The end
will come when God directly intervenes for Israel against
the actions of mankind.

The political and religious rejection of Israel will eventually result in a worldwide military attack on the nation.
The Bible describes at least three future wars which are
going to be beyond anything the world has ever seen before. Each war will get progressively greater and greater

until the last, known as Armageddon, involves all the nations of the world. The wars involving Israel are going to be greater in magnitude than World War II.

The future wars involving Israel are going to be cataclysmic. These wars will result in entire nations being destroyed and uninhabitable. Huge armies are going to be annihilated. The Bible says the last war will kill one-third of mankind. With today's world population of six billion, that would equal two billion people! Imagine a world war which kills two billion people!

The world events are now pointing to a huge confrontation with Islamic nations in the Middle East and other parts of the world. There will be no escaping the confrontation which is about to happen in the Middle East. The scenario painted by the Bible could easily be triggered by the confrontation building between Islamic nations and Israel. The entire world will be affected by this confrontation. The flow of oil out of the Middle East is very delicate and a catastrophic war could overnight cripple the world's oil supply. The stock markets and banks would be sent reeling from a massive war in the Middle East. It would be impossible for the nations of the world not to be drastically affected by a catastrophic war over Israel. A devastating war between Israel and the Islamic countries would destabilize the entire world. It seems the world is now rushing toward such a meltdown.

The fuse was lit on September 28, 2000, when Israeli general Ariel Sharon visited the Temple Mount in Jerusalem and vicious fighting erupted. The Muslims rioted over his presence on the Temple Mount site. This was the beginning of the Al-Aksa *intifada*. The Al-Aksa Mosque is located on the Temple Mount, and it is one of the most important religious sites in Islam. Ground zero for this fighting is the Temple Mount in Jerusalem. Exactly as the Bible so clearly states, Jerusalem has become a burdensome stone for all the nations of the world. "And in that day will I make Jerusalem a burdensome stone for all people: all that burden themselves with it shall be cut in pieces, though all the people of the earth be gathered together against it" (Zechariah 12:3). The fighting accelerated on September 11, 2001, with the Islamic terrorist attack on the World Trade Center (WTC) in New York City and the Pentagon. Both events have locked the world into a course of war. The vicious fighting which erupted in September 2000 has locked the Israelis and the Palestinians into a point of no return. The attack on the WTC has locked the U.S. into the point of no return with Islamic terrorist nations such as Afghanistan, Iraq, Sudan, Iran and Syria. It is highly possible the fuse which was lit on September 28, 2000, might explode into World War III. The potential is certainly there.

The attack on the United States seems to have abruptly changed the course of history. The attack and total destruction of the WTC took about ninety minutes, but the effect will go well into the future. It seems that September 11, 2001, was a day that created a line of demarcation in history. There seems to be no turning back from this event. The United States was drawn into a conflict with radical Islam and the states which support terrorism.

It is very possible with the biological, chemical, and possibly nuclear weapons that many terrorist supporting countries have, the incredible events outlined in the Bible could soon take place. The potential for mass destruction is at the fingertips of ruthless people. There are flash points all over the world. Any of these flash points could result in horrific wars which could escalate to draw in many other countries. Flash points such as Korea, Taiwan, Kashmir, and Jerusalem could ignite the use of weapons of mass destruction.

The catalyst for this massive attack against Israel will be Jerusalem. All the nations of the world will be drawn to Jerusalem in the final world war. Right now, Jerusalem is a sensitive issue to the nations of the world. The U.N. General Assembly voted in 1997 to condemn Israel for building a sixty-five hundred unit apartment complex on a barren hill in East Jerusalem. The U.N. voted 134–3 to condemn Israel for building this complex. It sounds bizarre that the U.N. would attempt to be involved in the building plans in the capital of an independent nation, but Jerusalem is not like any other city of the world. Jerusalem is unique because it is the city God has chosen as His own. Just as the Bible states, Jerusalem is the center of world attention.

In October 1991, former President George W. H. Bush started the Madrid peace process in an attempt to bring a regional peace to the Middle East. The heart of the plan was for Israel to give land for peace. In September 1993, Israel and the Palestinians agreed to the Oslo peace accords in an attempt to bring peace. The Oslo accords were a seven-year plan for Israel to give the Palestinians sections of the covenant land for peace.

In July 2000, former President William Clinton made a last ditch effort to conclude the Oslo peace accords. He had Israeli prime minister Ehud Barak and Palestinian leader Yasser Arafat meet for what became known as the Camp David summit. The effort failed over one key issue which was the control over Jerusalem and the Temple Mount. On July 20, 2000, the Associated Press reported about the stalled summit. In an article titled "Jerusalem At the Heart of the Mideast Talks," the article reported the following:

♦ "It seems the Israelis do not understand how important and sensitive the Jerusalem issue is to the Palestinians. . . . I believe the stubborn Israeli position is a call for another war. It is a tempting invitation to all fanatics and suicide bombers to act in order to save Jerusalem." (Ziad Abu Zayyad, Palestinian minister of Jerusalem)

 • "I held many talks with the Palestinians, and they think that we can and are willing to give up sovereignty in Jerusalem in general and the Old City in particular. I told them dream on." (Haim Ramon, Israeli minister of Jerusalem)

On July 26, 2000, the Associated Press reported in an article entitled "Peace Talks Collapse Over Jerusalem" why the summit failed. The article stated, "The chief cause of the breakdown, all sides said, was Jerusalem, which both sides claim as their capital."

Almost exactly two months later on September 28, on the Jewish holiday of Rosh Hashanah, fighting broke out on the Temple Mount over Jerusalem. The Palestinians decided to go to war with Israel over the covenant land and Jerusalem. The fighting and terrorist attacks against Israel have been nonstop. The battle over Jerusalem had begun.

The prophet Zechariah speaks so clearly about the military power of the reborn Israel. Israel will be an awesome power when the Jews are back in control of Jerusalem. Tiny Israel, the size of New Jersey, with five million Jews, is now one of the world's military powers. Israel has the finest air force in the world. Its army is superb. The nation has powerful nuclear weapons with the devastating Jericho missile delivery system that could destroy the entire Middle East. The Merkava tank and Israel's electronic warfare are also among the best in the world. Israel is truly a military power which is able to devour all the nations round about it. This is exactly what the Bible states Israel is to be like when the Jews return and control Jerusalem.

> In that day will I make the governors of Judah like an hearth of fire among the wood, and like a torch of fire in a sheaf; and they shall devour all the people round about, on the right hand and on the left: and Jerusalem shall be inhabited again in her own place, even in Jerusalem.
>
> —Zechariah 12:6

The nations of Egypt, Syria, and Iraq, plus the terrorist group Hamas in Lebanon all threatened to attack Israel if the fighting with the Palestinians escalated into a full scale war. The fighting over Jerusalem is on course for a regional war. The nations of Egypt, Iraq, and Syria are all identified in the Bible to be destroyed.

In March 2001, Egyptian president Hosni Mubarak visited President George W. Bush. While in Washington, he was interviewed by *Newsweek* magazine regarding the fighting between the Israelis and Palestinians. In an article entitled "It Is Out of Control," Mubarak said this about the fighting in Israel:

> Let me tell you, the most dangerous issue is not this. It's Jerusalem. Jerusalem can stop everything. . . . I don't think he [Arafat] will accept. Jerusalem is one reason. . . . You cannot imagine what public opinion was like here. I had warnings, don't ever sign anything concerning Jerusalem and the holy places.

The Islamic nations are all now being drawn to Jerusalem. All the world is focusing on Israel and the Middle East. Exactly as the Bible reported, Jerusalem is the focus of world attention and fighting. The fighting over Jerusalem has the potential to destabilize the entire world. What other city of the world could have this effect on the world? None! What is so amazing about the Bible is, you can read the prophet Zechariah, written about twenty-five hundred years ago; compare him with today's newspaper and Zechariah is reporting the same thing, the fighting over Jerusalem.

> Behold, I will make Jerusalem a cup of trembling unto all the people round about, when they shall be in the siege both against Judah and against Jerusalem. And in that day will I make Jerusalem a burdensome stone for all people: all that burden themselves with it shall be cut in pieces, though all the people of the earth be gathered together against it. . . .
>
> —Zechariah 12:2–3

Day of the Lord

> Blow ye the trumpet in Zion, and sound an alarm in my holy mountain: let all the inhabitants of the land tremble: for the day of the LORD cometh, for it is nigh at hand; A day of darkness and of gloominess, a day of clouds and of thick darkness, as the morning spread upon the mountains.
>
> —Joel 2:1–2

The phrase "day of the Lord" is one of the major prophetic themes of the Bible. A major portion of the Book of Revelation deals with the day of the Lord. The prophets Isaiah, Ezekiel, Joel, Obadiah, Zephaniah, Zechariah, and others all describe the events taking place during the day of the Lord. By looking at these prophets, a clear picture develops of what happens during the day of the Lord.

What Is the Day of the Lord?
The day of the Lord is a period of time which begins with

God's judgment on the world for rejecting Him. It is the time when God will interfere in the affairs of man in one last attempt to reach man before eternal judgment. Israel and Jerusalem will play a key role in the day of the Lord. The day of the Lord will continue through the awesome second coming of the Lord Jesus. It will include His thousand-year reign from Jerusalem as King.

The judgment part of the day of the Lord involves two phases. The first phase involves incredible wars. These wars lead up to a total world war which culminates in the battle of Armageddon. The wars are compressed into a short time period around seven to ten years. The prophet Zechariah goes into detail about the wars occurring during the day of the Lord. This final war will center around Jerusalem and all the nations of the world will be involved. "Behold, the day of the LORD cometh, and thy spoil shall be divided in the midst of thee. For I will gather all nations against Jerusalem to battle . . ." (Zechariah 14:1–2).

The second involves natural disasters which affect the entire world. The disasters include earthquakes, fires, famines, and pestilence. The earthquakes during this period are so massive they level the cities of the world. The judgment part of the day of the Lord is going to be a short but very intense period of time.

> Behold, the day of the LORD cometh, cruel both with wrath and fierce anger, to lay the land desolate: and he shall destroy the sinners thereof out of it. For the stars of heaven and the constellations thereof shall not give their light: the sun shall be darkened in his going forth, and the moon shall not cause her light to shine.
>
> —Isaiah 13:9–10

The wars and natural disasters are all happening simultaneously in this short time period. The breathtaking timing of natural disasters that have hit America is a warning of things to come. These disasters were in conjunction with events during which the U.S. pressured Israel. All this is a foreshadowing of what is going to happen during the day of the Lord. The day of the Lord will climax with the greatest war in history and with the greatest earthquake.

> For they are the spirits of devils, working miracles, which go forth unto the kings of the earth and of the whole world, to gather them to the battle of that great day of God Almighty. Behold, I come as a thief. Blessed is he that watcheth, and keepeth his garments, lest he walk naked, and they see his shame. And he gathered them together into a place called in the Hebrew tongue Armageddon. And the seventh angel poured out his vial into the air; and there came a great voice out of the temple of heaven, from the throne, saying, It is done. And there were voices, and thunders, and lightnings; and there was a great earthquake, such as was not since men were upon the earth, so mighty an earthquake, and so great.
>
> —Revelation 16:14–18

The day of the Lord will be the time God holds people accountable for rejecting Him for false gods and religions. It will be a time when God deals with the pride and rebellion of man. It is a reality check. Mankind for the most part lives apart from God. During the day of the Lord, the pride of man will be dealt with. The heart of man will be exposed to show how evil it is with wars and killing on a scale never before seen. God will let man's evil heart have its way, and then bring judgment on the actions. Through it all God always has the way of salvation open to Him.

During the day of the Lord many will repent and turn to the Lord Jesus as they see there is no hope outside of trusting God. God is using this time to bring man to his senses. Everything that can be shaken will be shaken. Only that which is of God is going to stand in the future.

> And I will punish the world for their evil, and the wicked for their iniquity; and I will cause the arrogancy of the proud to cease, and will lay low the haughtiness of the terrible. I will make a man more precious than fine gold; even a man than the golden wedge of Ophir.
>
> —Isaiah 13:11–12

It appears the worldwide war phase of the day of the Lord as described by the ancient prophets is now coming together with rapid speed. Nation after nation have armed with weapons of mass destruction. The United States, Russia, China, and Israel all have huge arsenals of these fearful weapons and are getting more powerful each day. India and Pakistan have both developed nuclear weapons and have threatened to use them against each other. Terrorist nations such as Iran, Iraq, and Syria all have biological and chemical weapons and they are working around the clock to develop nuclear weapons. Think of nuclear weapons in the hands of the tyrants in the Middle East! How long before one of these nations has such a weapon? Iran and Iraq may already have nuclear weapons. Could the world be on the verge of the day of the Lord? Let us look at what the Bible describes as the day of the Lord and the events which are now transpiring.

There are certain indicators in the Bible which have to be in place for the day of the Lord to occur. These indicators are now in place. The setting is when the nation of Israel is reborn, but just before the second coming of the Lord Jesus. The Jews must return to Israel from a worldwide dispersion. Jerusalem must once again be the capital of Israel. Israel has to be a great military power. The nations of the world have to reject Israel. Russia must be a major military power. Asia must be able to field an army of two hundred million. Israel must be the subject of horrific wars.

God is now using the rebirth of the nation of Israel as His anvil to show the literalness and authority of His Word. The time is coming when God will use Israel as a physical anvil to judge the nations of the world. This will happen when the nations unite in the final stage of rebellion against God in an attempt to destroy Israel. This attack will be, in effect, to try and break God's covenant with Abraham, Isaac, and Jacob over the land. In great detail, the Bible describes what happens to these nations when they attempt to destroy Israel.

The Bible actually names many of the nations and describes their destruction. The unified world effort to try and destroy Israel will fail. Attacking Israel and Jerusalem is God's litmus test for judging the peoples and nations. The nations are judged as they attack Israel.

A nation represents the corporate thinking of the people. If the corporate attitude of a nation does not honor God's Word and covenants, then the leadership of this nation will reflect this thinking. The Islamic nations, which represent hundreds of millions of people, reject the nation of Israel. Communist China and India, which are primarily Hindu, reject that Israel is a covenant nation with God. The Islamic, Communist, and Hindu nations represent half the world's population. The so-called Christian nations are in deep apostasy away from the Word of God and reject the covenant. America seems to be the only nation with a part of the population which recognizes the covenant and stands with Israel. The nations of the world have rejected God, His Word, and His covenant with Israel. This rebellion against God will culminate in what the Bible calls the battle of Armageddon, the final battle for Jerusalem.

This rejection of Israel is nearly complete. Nearly all the world power centers are against Israel. The U.N. continually votes against Israel. Usually, the United States is the only nation that votes with Israel. America took a huge turn in October 2001 by stating the U.S. would recognize a Palestinian state with East Jerusalem as the capital. The last bastion of support for Israel was drying up. The U.S. forcing Israel to accept a Palestinian state would complete the world scene. Israel would be left to trust only on God for its survival.

Chapter 13

The Third War—Armageddon

And he gathered them together into a place called in the
Hebrew tongue Armageddon.

—Revelation 16:16

A noise shall come even to the ends of the earth; for the
LORD hath a controversy with the nations, he will plead
with all flesh; he will give them that are wicked to the
sword, saith the LORD.

—Jeremiah 25:31

One expression from the Bible that almost everyone
has heard is Armageddon. This will be the final battle
between evil and God. Armageddon is not a battle between
good and evil on earth. It is the battle where God Himself
directly intervenes and destroys the largest army in history. These armies are attempting to destroy Israel and take
Jerusalem.

The final war will be fought over Jerusalem. God is using Jerusalem as a lure and the people in rebellion against
Him will come literally by the hundred of millions. The
prophet Zechariah shows the final battle before the second
coming of the Lord Jesus will be over Jerusalem. All the
nations will be drawn to Jerusalem.

+ Zechariah 14:1–2: "Behold, the day of the LORD
cometh, and thy spoil shall be divided in the midst of

thee. For I will gather all nations against Jerusalem to battle; and the city shall be taken, and the houses rifled, and the women ravished; and half of the city shall go forth into captivity, and the residue of the people shall not be cut off from the city."

♦ Joel 3:2: "I will also gather all nations, and will bring them down into the valley of Jehoshaphat, and will plead [judge] with them there for my people and for my heritage Israel, whom they have scattered among the nations, and parted my land."

All of man's rebellion against God will culminate at this battle over Jerusalem. During the previous battles, there is no indication from Scripture that Jerusalem was overrun. In this final battle, an army of two hundred million invade the Middle East. This huge army comes from Asia. All of Asia will be at this battle, along with the other nations of the world. Asia will be unified as the army marches to Israel. The apostle John in the Book of Revelation states this army will number two hundred million.

> Saying to the sixth angel which had the trumpet, Loose the four angels which are bound in the great river Euphrates. And the four angels were loosed, which were prepared for an hour, and a day, and a month, and a year, for to slay the third part of men. And the number of the army of the horsemen were two hundred thousand thousand [two hundred million]: and I heard the number of them. . . . By these three was the third part of men killed, by the fire, and by the smoke, and by the brimstone, which issued out of their mouths.
>
> —Revelation 9:14–18

The Euphrates River is the traditional dividing line between the Middle East and Asia. This army is going to cross the

Euphrates River and pour into the Middle East. On the way to Jerusalem it is going to spread into other nations and a third of mankind will be killed. The Bible says this army is led by the unified kings of the East or Asia.

> And the sixth angel poured out his vial upon the great river Euphrates; and the water thereof was dried up, that the way of the kings of the east might be prepared. . . . For they are the spirits of devils, working miracles, which go forth unto the kings of the earth and of the whole world, to gather them to the battle of that great day of God Almighty. Behold, I come as a thief. Blessed is he that watcheth, and keepeth his garments, lest he walk naked, and they see his shame. And he gathered them together into a place called in the Hebrew tongue Armageddon.
>
> —Revelation 16:12–16

China, combined with the rest of Asia, could field an army of this size. China has been undertaking a huge military buildup in recent years. It appears that in the near future, Asia will be united under China. The United States has been the major Asian power since World War II. In the near future, the power of the U.S. will have to be broken to allow all of Asia to be unified under China. The rapid buildup of China and the possible war at any time between North and South Korea could destabilize Asia. America might not be able to defend South Korea and Taiwan if tied up in a war with Islamic terrorist nations.

The Future of America

For Bible prophecy about the war of Gog-Magog and Armageddon to be fulfilled, something has to have happened to the world power and influence of the United States.

American military power and NATO would block any attempt by Russia to form a coalition and invade Israel. For this to happen, America has to cease being a world power in the Middle East. There has to be a tremendous shift away from American power.

For the countries of Asia to unite in a massive army that will be present at Armageddon, something has to happen to American power in Asia. At the present time, the U.S. is the block for this to happen. For all of Asia to be united, America has to cease as an Asian world power. Taiwan will have to be reunited with China and North Korea has to overcome the South.

The future for the United States looking through Bible prophecy is not good. America has been warned by God over and over again with warning-judgments about abortion and homosexuality. The U.S. policy has destabilized Israel, God's covenant nation. America has done everything to bring God's judgment. It appears that God is going to remove America from being a world power because of the national sin and rebellion against Him. If the events we are witnessing are the start of the day of the Lord, then America's time as a super power is very short. God in His mercy has warned and warned of the coming judgment, but the church has failed to recognize the warnings and lead the nation in repentance before God.

If America's power was broken in Asia, no country could stand against China. Japan, Philippines, Indonesia, Australia, and the rest of Asia would quickly fall under Chinese control. China has nuclear missiles and no country could resist the military might of China. All Asia would very quickly come under Chinese control if the United States was removed as an Asian power.

A move of China westward could start a nuclear war with Russia. If Russia and the United States have been removed as world powers, China with the rest of Asia could move freely westward as the Bible says one day is going to happen. This move of China will lead directly to Jerusalem and Armageddon.

The battle of Armageddon will spread down to Jerusalem. The fighting will be so awful that the Bible says it will be the wine press of the wrath of God.

> And the angel thrust in his sickle into the earth, and gathered the vine of the earth, and cast it into the great winepress of the wrath of God. And the winepress was trodden without the city, and blood came out of the winepress, even unto the horse bridles, by the space of a thousand and six hundred furlongs.
>
> —Revelation 14:19–20

Man's evil nature will be unrestrained during this time. The killing will be endless as man is left to his nature. God will use His covenant nation Israel as His anvil. God will use Israel to reveal His mighty power. The day of the Lord will be the time when the peoples of the earth get exactly what they deserve. God is totally just, and during this time, mankind will be given exactly what is just. "For the day of the Lord is near upon all the heathen: as thou hast done, it shall be done unto thee: thy reward shall return upon thine own head" (Obadiah 1:15).

His Feet Shall Stand in That Day

The battle of Armageddon will end with the literal second coming of the Lord Jesus. The earth will not be totally destroyed and everyone killed. God will not let this happen, nor will He allow man to totally destroy himself and the world. This battle will lead to the near destruction of Jerusalem and the covenant land. The entire earth is going to be in an upheaval at this time. There will be massive natural disasters in addition to the wars. When the Lord returns, it will not be to New York, London, or Mecca. He will return to Jerusalem. His coming will trigger a massive earthquake.

> Behold, the day of the LORD cometh, and thy spoil shall be divided in the midst of thee. For I will gather all nations against Jerusalem to battle; and the city shall be taken, and the houses rifled, and the women ravished; and half of the city shall go forth into captivity, and the residue of the people shall not be cut off from the city. Then shall the LORD go forth, and fight against those nations, as when he fought in the day of battle. And his feet shall stand in that day upon the mount of Olives, which is before Jerusalem on the east, and the mount of Olives shall cleave in the midst thereof toward the east and toward the west, and there shall be a very great valley; and half of the mountain shall remove toward the north, and half of it toward the south.
>
> —Zechariah 14:1–4

From the natural human perspective, man is hurtling toward Armageddon. From God's perspective, He is getting ready for the second coming of the Lord Jesus and to end evil. From the natural perspective, there will be no hope. From God's perspective, it will be the beginning of a new era on earth.

Armageddon will be the perfect picture of how evil the heart of man is apart from God. Armageddon will trigger the second coming of the Lord. He will defend the land of His everlasting covenant and His people Israel. The presence of the Lord in His glory and the power of His spoken Word will destroy the armies against Israel. The effect of God's spoken Word against rebellious man will be like a neutron bomb. The war will be instantly over at the Lord's second coming.

> And this shall be the plague wherewith the LORD will smite all the people that have fought against Jerusalem; Their flesh shall consume away while they stand upon their feet, and their eyes shall consume away in their holes, and their tongue shall consume away in their mouth.
>
> —Zechariah 14:12

Israel failed to recognize Jesus at His first coming, but will understand at His second coming. The events leading up to Armageddon will have opened the eyes of Israel to God. God is going to use these wars to bring Israel to the understanding that Jesus was pierced on the cross for Israel as well as all people. It will be a time for mourning and reconciliation with their Messiah. Israel will be reunited with the Lord Jesus.

> And it shall come to pass in that day, that I will seek to destroy all the nations that come against Jerusalem. And I will pour upon the house of David, and upon the inhabitants of Jerusalem, the spirit of grace and of supplications: and they shall look upon me whom they have pierced, and they shall mourn for him, as one mourneth for his only son, and shall be in bitterness for him, as one that is in bitterness for his firstborn.
>
> —Zechariah 12:9–10

The Bible Is the Word of God

> The words of the LORD are pure words: as silver tried in a furnace of earth, purified seven times. Thou shalt keep them, O LORD, thou shalt preserve them from this generation for ever.
>
> —Psalm 12:6–7

The authority of the Bible can be seen with the nation of Israel. The prophets from thousands of years ago speak directly to today. What people are like the Jews and what nation like Israel? What book is like the Bible? You can test the authority of the Bible with Israel. Everything the prophets said about Israel is being fulfilled right before our eyes. How could a book written by mere men do this? The words of the prophets have been tested in a furnace of earth and have been found to be pure.

Israel was always a small nation, and it never was a great empire like Rome. All the ancient empires have long been destroyed, but Israel was reborn. All those empires with tremendous armies and wealth are gone. Israel should have ceased to exist in 586 B.C. and definitely in A.D. 70. But Israel is not like any other nation, Israel exists because of a covenant God made with Abraham four thousand years ago. The effect of the covenant can be seen today. Israel is once again a nation, with Jerusalem as its capital. Just as the Bible so clearly states, Jerusalem is a burdensome stone for all the nations. Huge regional wars leading to world wars can start over Jerusalem.

The entire prophetic picture painted by the ancient prophets of the Bible is focusing right before our eyes. Only a book given directly by God could so accurately foretell the history of Israel leading up to today. The near future is there in the Bible for all to read. The breathtaking timing of the judgments on America for forcing Israel over the covenant land are forewarning to the nations of the world what will happen during the day of the Lord. America has been dealt with exactly like the Bible says will happen to any nation that tries to interfere with the everlasting covenant.

God's Word has been truly proven in the furnace of the earth. It is there for all to see. God has done all this with

Israel out in the open for all to see. Nothing has been hidden by God or done in secret. God is bringing the fulfillment of His prophetic plan for the second coming of His Son right before the eyes of the entire world. It is all out in the open. The Bible speaks about more than Israel. It tells of a literal heaven and hell and eternal life. It talks about mankind being separated from God by sin. It talks about God's love for man. It talks about forgiveness of sin and reconciliation with the holy God of Israel. It talks about God in the person of Jesus Christ dying on the cross to pay the price for sin. The authority of the Bible has been proven by the nation of Israel. Great attention should be paid to the complete message. According to the Bible, there is a literal heaven and a literal hell.

Awesome events of the day of the Lord seem to be right before us. Events which shall shake this world to its very foundation. God has given us a picture of the future. There is no doubt these things will happen just as described by the prophets. The event that is the most important is the second coming of the Son of God. Everything else—including Armageddon—pales in comparison. Are you ready to stand before the Lord Jesus?

> For God so loved the world, that he gave his only begotten Son, that whosoever believeth in him should not perish, but have everlasting life.
>
> —John 3:16

The Bible is the Word of God.

> **And I will bless them that bless thee, and curse him that curseth thee: and in thee shall all families of the earth be blessed.**
>
> —Genesis 12:3

Documentation

Chapter 6: America: Blessed or Cursed?

November 1991

Opening of Madrid Peace Talks: *New York Times,* October 31, 1991, front-page article titled "Israel and Arabs, Face to Face, Begin Quest for Mideast Peace."

Storm: *New York Times,* front-page article titled "Out of Clear Sky, Big Winds Swamp Shore." *USA Today,* November 1, 1997, front-page article titled "East Coast hit hard by rare storm." and "One-on-one peace talks to begin next."

The Land of Israel Key Issue: *New York Times,* October 31, 1991, article titled "Excerpts the Speeches in Madrid."

Storm Development and Madrid Conference: *New York Times,* November 1, 1997, front-page articles titled "Mideast Foes List Demands and Trade Angry Charges Across Conference Table" and "Nameless Storm Batters Northeast Again."

Storm traveled 1,000 miles the wrong way: *New York Times,* November 1, 1997, article titled "Nameless Storm Swamps the Shoreline."

President Bush's Home Smashed by the Storm: *New York Times,* November 1, 1997, article titled "Story Waves Heavily Damage Bush Vacation Compound in Southern Maine."

The Perfect Storm: Book titled *The Perfect Storm* by Sebastian Junger, 1997, W. W. Norton & Co.

Facts About the Storm: CNN, June 30, 2001, article titled "The actual 'Perfect Storm': A perfectly dreadful combination of nature's forces."

August 1992

Statement made by Acting Secretary of Eagleburger: *New York Times,* August 24, 1992, article titled "Politics Just Might Help Mideast Talks."

Hurricane Andrew and Madrid Peace Plan Together: *New York Times,* August 26, 1992, articles titled " Thousands Homeless in Florida Storm," "Israel Offers Plan for Arabs to Rule in Occupied Lands," and "Bush's Gains from Convention Nearly Evaporate in Latest Poll." *USA Today,* August 24, 1992, front-page article titled "1 million flee Andrew" and "Mideast peace talks to resume on positive note."

Damage Done by Andrew: *USA Today,* September 14, 1992, article titled "Tale of the Hurricanes." *USA Today,* September 18, 1992, article titled "Andrew 3rd-worst storm."

September 1993

Hurricane Emily and Dividing the Land of Israel: *New York Times,* September 1, 1993, front-page articles (these articles touched each other) titled: "Israel and PLO Ready to Declare Joint Recognition" and "Hurricane Hits the Outer Banks, As Thousands Seek Safety Inland."

January 1994

President Clinton and Assad meet in Geneva: *New York Times*, January 17, 1994, front-page article titled "Assad Holds Out Prospect of Normal Ties with Israel after Talks with Clinton."

Earthquake in L.A.: *Los Angeles Times*, January 18, 1994, front-page article titled "33 Die, Many Hurt in 6.6 Quake."

The earthquake was two at the same time: *USA Today*, January 26, 1994, article titled "Quake packed a one-two punch."

Fault that caused the quake no found: *USA Today*, November 31, 1994, article titled "Experts try to put a face on no-name fault."

Quake destroys the pornography center of USA: Associated Press, January 28, 1994, article titled "Quake affects porn industry."

March 1997

Arafat arrives in America and meets with Clinton and massive destruction in Arkansas: *New York Times*, March 4, 1997, front-page articles titled "Welcoming Arafat, Clinton Rebukes Israel" and "In Storms' Wake Grief and Shock."

Magnitude of the Storm: *USA Today*, March 3, 1997, front-page article titled "Tornadoes, flooding kill 42."

Damage Done by Storm: *USA Today*, March 10, 1997, article titled "The Damage."

Clinton Returns to Arkansas: *New York Times*, March 5, 1997, front-page article titled "Clinton Goes Home and Finds State Crushed By Storm."

Arafat on speaking tour: *New York Times*, March 6, 1997, article titled "Arafat Lobbies U.S. Against Israel's Housing Plan."

Security Counsel's Resolution of March 6, 1997: *New York Times*, March 7, 1997, article titled "U.S. Vetoes U.N. Criticism of Israel's Construction Plan."

General Assembly Resolution of March 13, 1997: *New York Times*, March 14, 1997, article titled "Israel's Plan of Jerusalem Is Condemned by Assembly."

Security Counsel's Resolution of March 21, 1997: New York Times, March 22, 1997, article titled "U.S. Again Vetoes a Move by U.N. Condemning Israel."

General Assembly Resolution of April 25, 1997: *New York Times*, April 25, 1997, article titled "Israel Warned to Halt Housing for Jews."

General Assembly Resolution of July 15, 1997: *New York Times*, July 16, 1997, article titled "U.N. Renews Censure of New Israeli Housing in East Jerusalem."

Stock Market Reaches All Time High: *USA Today*, March 12, 1997, article titled "Dow achieves record despite rate fears."

Stock Market Falls 160 Points: *USA Today*, March 14, 1997, article titled "Dow plunges 160 points on rate fears."

Stock Market Stabilizes and Begins Rebound: *USA Today*, April 15, 1997, article titled "Stock Market Summary."

Prime Minister Netanyahu Meets with Clinton: *New York Times*, April 8, 1997, article titled "Netanyahu Holds White House Talks."

July 1997

Devaluation of Thailand's Currency: *New York Times*, July 2, 1997, article titled "Thais Effectively Devalue Their Wobbly Currency."

U.N. Resolution July 15, 1997: *New York Times*, July 16, 1997, article titled "U.N. Renews Censure of New Israeli Housing in East Jerusalem."

Stock Market Crash: *New York Times*, October 27, 1997, article titled "Stocks Fall 554 Points, Off 7% Forcing Suspension in Trading."

Asian Crisis Affects World Economy: *USA Today*, October 24, 1997, article titled "Market dive circles globe."

January 1998

Clinton meets with Netanyahu: *New York Times*, January 22, 1998, article titled, "U.S. and Israel Talk Mainly of More Talks." *USA Today*, January 22, 1998, article titled, "A Mideast battle for good press."

Clinton meets with Arafat: *USA Today*, January 23, 1998, article titled, "Arafat calls talks encouraging."

Clinton's sex scandal breaks during meeting with Netanyahu: *New York Times*, January 22, 1998, front-page article titled "Subpoenas Sent as Clinton Denies Reports of an Affair with Aide at White House."

Clinton coldly treats Netanyahu and Netanyahu returns as a hero: *New York Times*, January 30, 1998, article titled "Analysis: In Clinton Crisis, Netanyahu Gains, Arafat Loses"

House votes to begin impeachment of president: Associated Press, October 8, 1998, article titled "House Approves Impeachment Inquiry."

September 1998

Clinton to meet with Netanyahu and Arafat: *New York Times*, September 25, 1998, article titled "Clinton to See Netanyahu and Arafat Next Week."

Hurricane gains strength: *USA Today*, September 25, 1998, front-page article titled "Georges gaining strength: Killer storm zeros in on Key West."

Secretary of State Albright meets with Arafat in New York City: *New York Times*, September 28, 1998, article titled "US Is Hoping to Announce Details on Israel-Palestine Talks."

Hurricane Georges slams into Gulf Coast: *New York Times*, September 28, 1998, front-page article titled "Recharged Hurricane Batters Gulf Coast with 110 M.P.H. Winds."

Hurricane Lingers on Gulf Coast: *USA Today*, September 29, 1998, front-page article titled "Georges Lingers."

President Clinton meets with Arafat and Netanyahu in White House: *USA Today*, September 29, 1998, front-page article titled "Meeting puts Mideast talks back in motion."

Hurricane and Mideast peace talks together: *New York Times*, September 29, 1998, front-pages articles titled "U.S., Israel and Arafat Inch Toward Pact" and "Floods Trap Hundreds."

Arafat speaks at United Nations: *New York Times*, September 29, 1998, article titled "Arafat, at U.N., Urges Backing for Statehood."

Hurricane causes $1 billion in damage: *USA Today*, September 30, 1998, article titled "Hurricane racks up $1 billion in damage."

October 1998

Netanyahu and Arafat met in United States: *Harrisburg Patriot News*, October 15, 1998, front-page article titled "Time is running out in Mideast."

Israel to give away 13 percent of the land: *New York Times*, October 24, 1998, front-page article titled "Arafat and Netanyahu in Pact on Next Steps Toward Peace; Modest Deal to Rebuild Trust."

Powerful storms hit Texas: *Harrisburg Patriot News*, October 18, 1998, article titled "4 killed as storms, floods tornado ravage parts of Texas."

Extent of the flooding and damage: *New York Times*, October 20, 1998, article titled "Record Flooding Kills at Least 14 in Central Texas." *USA Today*, October 22, 1998, article titled "Hope dwindles in flooded Texas."

Texas declared a disaster area by president: Federal Emergency Management Agency (FEMA) news release dated October 21, 1998, titled "President Declares Major Disaster for Texas: Twenty Counties Designated for Aid to Flood Victims."

This disaster and Mideast talks together on front page of newspaper: *New York Times*, October 20, 1998, articles titled "Clinton Keeps Up Hope of Mideast Talks" and "Knee-deep in the San Jacinto."

November 1998

Stock Market reached all time high on November 23, 1998: Associated Press News Service, December 10, 1998, article titled "Stocks fall for third straight session."

Clinton and Arafat met on November 30 to raise money for Palestinians: *Baltimore Sun*, December 1, 1998, front-page article titled "Nations pledge $3 billion in aid to Palestinians."

Stock market drops 216 points on November 30: *Baltimore Sun*, December 1, 1998, front-page article titled "Expected correction cools off Wall St." (The articles about Arafat and the stock market were next to each other on the front page.)

European stock markets crash: Associated Press News Service, December 2, 1998, article titled "UK stocks hammered."

December 1998

Judicial committee votes on December 11 for three articles of impeachment: *USA Today*, December 11, 1998, front-page article titled "Panel
sets stage for historic vote on impeachment."

Clinton en route to Israel while the fourth article of impeachment is being voted: Associated Press News Service, December 12, 1998, articles titled "Clinton Heads for Israel" and "Fourth Impeachment Article Debated."

Clinton is the first president to visit Palestinian controlled area: *USA Today*, December 12, 1998, front-page article titled "Clinton fights for
Mideast agreement."

Clinton's visit gives status to a Palestinian state: *USA Today*, December
12, 1998, front-page article titled "Peace hits snag despite vote."

On December 19 Clinton impeached by the House of Representatives:
Sunday Patriot-News, Harrisburg, Pa., December 20, 1998, front-page
article titled "Impeached."

March 1999

President Clinton meets with Arafat: *New York Times*, March 24, 1999,
article titled "Arafat Says Little on Clinton Meeting."

Dow takes big fall: *Washington Post*, March 24, 1999, article titled "Dow
Takes Biggest Fall in 2 Months."

USA attacks Serbia: *Washington Post*, March 25, 1999, front-page article
titled "US, Allies Launch Air Attack on Yugoslav Military Targets."

Russian statements about WW3: *Boston Globe*, April 8, 1999, article titled
"Russian Military Sees a Balkan Opportunity."

Dangers of Sino-Russian alliance: *NewsMax.com*, November 19, 2000,
article titled "Sino-Russian Alliance Threatens U.S. Global Policies."
Washington Post, November 25, 2000, article titled "House reports
warns of anti-U.S. alliance."

May 1999

Tornado warnings: *USA Today*, May 5, 1999, article titled "Sky's darkwall
of death leaves nowhere to run."

Speed of winds: *USA Today*, May 11, 1999, article titled "318 mph storm
wind fastest ever."

Newspaper headlines: *USA Today*, May 5, 1999, front-page article titled
"Everything was gone." *Harrisburg Patriot-News*, May 5, 1999, front-
page article titled "20 hours of terror." *Daily Oklahoma*, May 5, 1999,
front-page article titled "Stark Scene: Miles of Destruction."

Statements by Governor Frank Keating: *USA Today*, May 5, 1999, article
titled "Disasters declared in two states."

May 4,1999, Arafat was declare a state: *Omaha World-Herald*, May 4,
1999, article titled "Mideast Deadline Passes."

President Bush encourages Arafat about Palestinian state: Associated
Press, May 4, 1999, article titled "Clinton Encourages Arafat."

Clinton declares two states disaster areas: *USA Today*, May 5, 1999, article titled "Disasters declared in two states."

September 1999

Hurricane Dennis: *USA Today*, September 2, 1999, article titled "Dennis makes comeback, blasts Outer Banks." *New York Times*, September 3, 1999, article titled "Weakened Storm Worse Than a Hurricane, Geologist Says." Associated Press, September 3, 1999, article titled "Dennis Continues to Menace N.C."

Secretary of State Albright meets with Arab leaders: *New York Times*, September 3, 1999, front-page article titled "Mideast Standoff Remains Unsolved as Albright Visits."

Hurricane Dennis hits as Albright meets with Arafat: *Harrisburg Patriot-News*, September 4, 1999, front-page articles titled "Enough already: N.C. tires of Dennis" and "Talks yield reworking of Wye pact."

Final Status meeting: Associated Press, September 13, 1999, article titled "Israel, Palestinians to Open Talks."

Hurricane Floyd strengthens: Associated Press, September 13, 1999, article titled "Floyd Strengthens, Near Bahamas."

Devastation of Hurricane Floyd: *Harrisburg Patriot-News*, September 19, 1999, front-page article titled "Floodwaters devastating N. Carolina."

Stock market losses: Reuters, September 23, 1999, article titled "Dow, Nasdaq Take Late-Day Tumble."

Arafat visits Clinton: Associated Press, September 22, 1999, article titled "Clinton Hosts Arafat at White House."

October 1999

Eviction of fifteen settlements: Associated Press, October 13, 1999, article titled "Jewish Settlers Protest Evacuation."

Hurricane Irene: *USA Today*, October 16, 1999, article titled "Battered North Carolina suffers third hurricane in two months."

Earthquake: *Los Angeles Times*, October 17, 1999, front-page article titled "7.0 Earthquake in Mojave Desert Rocks Southland."

Faults said "conversating:" Associated Press, October 19, 1999, article titled "Quake Fault Lines Said Conversating."

January 2000

Meeting between President Clinton, Barak and al Shara: *USA Today*, January 4, 2000, front-page article titled "Deal markers go to work." *New York Times*, January 4, 2000, front-page article titled "Israel and Syria Return to Search For Major Accord."

Israel and Syria continue meeting: *USA Today*, January 5, 2000, article titled "Negotiators clear first bump in Middle East talks."

Stock market collapses: *USA Today*, January 5, 2000, front-page article titled "Market sell-off was overdue."

March 10, 2000

Israel to offer a Palestinian state: Associated Press, March 11, 2000, article titled "Israel to make offer, report says."

Nasdaq index reaches all time high: *New York Times*, March 11, 2000, article titled "Nasdaq Is Barely Higher; Other Indexes Close Down."

President Clinton summons PM Barak to Washington: Associated Press, April 12, 2000, article titled "Israel OKs US Involvement in Talks."

Stock market collapse: *USA Today*, April 11–13, 2000, articles titled "Tech worries topple Nasdaq," "Market punishes tech's bad news," and "Nasdaq plunges again."

Nasdaq fell 618 points for the week: *New York Times*, April 15, 2000, front-page article titled "Stock Market in Steep Drop as Worried Investors Flee; Nasdaq Has Its Worst Week."

Arafat comes to Washington: Associated Press, June 15, 2000, article titled "Clinton welcomes Arafat for talks."

Stock market drop: Reuters, June 16, 2000, article titled "Banks Lead Blue Chip Plunge."

July–August 2000

Camp David meetings and collapse over Jerusalem: Associated Press, July 20, 2000, article titled "Jerusalem at Heart of Mideast Talks." Reuters, July 21, 2000, article titled "Jerusalem Sovereignty Debated in Public amid Talks." Associated Press, July 26, 2000, article titled "Peace Talks Collapse over Jerusalem."

Texas declared disaster area: Associated Press, July 28, 2000, article titled "Bush Declares Texas Disaster Areas."

Weather is "Perfect Storm" for fires: Reuters, August 27, 2000, article titled "U.S. Wildfires Converge in 'Perfect Storm.'"

Facts of the wildfires: *Washington Post*, August 7, 2000, article titled "Beast of a Fire Resists Taming By Elite Team." Associated Press, August 30, 2000, article titled "Wildfire Fight to Cost $1 Billion."

Record drought: Associated Press, August 27, 2000, article titled "Record-Tying Dry Spell Hits Texas."

September–December 2000

Fighting over the Temple Mount: *New York Times*, September 30, 2000, front-page article titled "Battle at Jerusalem Holy Site Leaves 4 Dead and 200 Hurt."

Clinton and Arafat meet: *New York Times*, November 10, 2000, article titled "Clinton Meets Arafat."

Israeli and U.S. governments destabilized: *Washington Post*, December 10, 2000, front-page articles titled "Divided US Supreme Court Orders Freeze on Fla. Count" and "Israeli Prime Minister Says He Will Resign."

Election in the Supreme Court: *New York Times*, December 11, 2000, front-page article titled "Bush v. Gore Is Now in the Hands of the Supreme Court."

June 2001
Tropical Storm Allison great rainfall: *Houston Chronicle*, June 10, 2001, article titled "Allison rivals Claudette's 79 record." *Houston Chronicle*, June 14, 2001, article titled "Mayor: Storm city's biggest disaster ever." President Bush declares five states disaster areas: Associated Press, June 23, 2001, article titled "Bush Releases $500M in Storm Aid."
Forming of Allison: *Houston Chronicle*, June 6, 2001, article titled "Tropical surprise floods area."
U.S. involvement in mediation in cease fire: Reuters, June 8, 2001, article titled "US Steps Up Middle East Peace Drive Amid Violence." Associated Press, June 9, 2001, article titled "US Steps Up Mideast Peace Efforts." *Jerusalem Post*, June 14, 2001, article titled "Settlers: Tenet plan amounts to our 'abandonment.'"

September 11, 2001
President Bush's speech on August 9, 2001: CNN, August 9, 2001, article titled "Bush condemns Jerusalem suicide bombing."
Tourist industry hurt: Cybercast News Service, *cnsnews.com*, dated October 15, 2001, article titled "Travel and Tourism Hurt by Fear of Flying."
U.S. to recognize a Palestinian state: *New York Times*, October 2, 2001, article titled "Before Attacks, US Was Ready to Say It Backed Palestinian State." *Washington Post*, October 2, 2001, article titled "US Was Set to Support Palestinian Statehood."

November 2001
The president's speech before the U.N.: *New York Times*, November 11, 2001, front-page article titled "All Must Join Fight Against Terror, Bush Tells UN."
Secretary of state meets with Arafat: *New York Times*, November 12, 2001, article titled "Arafat Thankful for Bush Remark about 'Palestine.'"
Powell says use of Palestine correct: Associated Press, November 11, 2001, article titled "Powell: Use of 'Palestine' Deliberate."
Rumsfield worried about nuke threat: News Max, *newsmax.com*, November 11, 2001, article titled "Rumsfield: 'Seriously Worried' about bin Laden Nuke Threat."
Jet crash from JFK: *New York Times*, November 13, 2001, front-page article titled "Jet with 260 Crashes in Queens; 6 to 9 Missing as 12 Homes Burn; US Doubts Link To Terrorism."

Links to Middle East U.N. Resolutions and Peace Covenants
United Nations Resolution 242, November 22, 1967
www.yale.edu/lawweb/avalon/un/un242.htm
United Nations Resolution 338, November 22, 1967
www.yale.edu/lawweb/avalon/un/un338.htm
Remarks at the opening session of the Middle East Peace Conference in

Madrid, Spain by President George H. W. Bush on October 30, 1991—
www.bushlibrary.tamu.edu/papers/1991/91103000.html
Oslo 1: Declaration of Principles on Interim Self-Government Arrangements, September 13, 1993—*www.israel.org/mfa/go.asp?MFAH00q00*
Olso 2: Treaty of Peace Between the State of Israel and the Hashemite Kingdom of Jordan, October 26, 1994—*www.israel.org/mfa/ go.asp?MFAH00pa0*
Wye River Memorandum, October 23, 1998
www.state.gov/www/regions/nea/981023_interim_agmt.html
The Mitchell Report on Israeli–Palestinian Violence, April 30, 2001—
www2.haaretz.co.il/breaking-news/kuku/362927.stm